E.L.M.

STRICT SETTLEMENT

University of Hull Press

Occasional Papers in Economic and Social History
No. 10

General Editor: John Saville
Emeritus Professor of Economic and Social History
in the University of Hull

STRICT SETTLEMENT

A Guide for Historians

BARBARA ENGLISH
Lecturer in Regional and Local History
University of Hull

and

JOHN SAVILLE
Emeritus Professor of Economic and Social History
University of Hull

UNIVERSITY OF HULL PRESS
1983

ISBN 0 85958 439 9

Phototypeset in 11 on 12 pt Baskerville
and Printed in England by
The Walkergate Press Limited
Wilbert Grove, Beverley, North Humberside

PREFACE

Historians and politicians have always been interested in the land question, in all its many aspects, and the subject matter of this monograph was of considerable political moment in the nineteenth century and has been of increasing historical concern in our own century.

Our purpose has been strictly defined: we have restricted ourselves to explication of the nature and character of the strict settlement in its multifarious expression, and we have not been in any way concerned with its economic, social and political consequences. We are naturally not unaware of the continuing debate on these matters, and the shape of our discussion has no doubt to some extent been moulded by the questions currently being raised; but for the most part we have deliberately eschewed these problems. We are historians writing for historians, and we have been acutely conscious of our lack of expertise in the difficult areas of legal history into which we have had to enter. While we have been much helped by our colleagues, lawyers and historians, we must make a more than formal disclaimer that our mistakes are our own responsibility.

We are grateful to those whose archives we have been allowed to consult: to the late Commander R. R. Bower, Mr John Chichester Constable, Lord Downe, Mr R. Heptonstall, Lord Hotham, the Earl of Leicester, Lord Middleton, the Duke of Newcastle, the trustees of the Saltmarshe estate, Miss Schofield and Sir Tatton Sykes Bt. The Master and Fellows of Downing College, Cambridge allowed us access to the College muniments and we were greatly helped by Mr Stanley French. Dr W. O. Hassall and Mrs Hiskey generously answered our questions about the Holkham archives; and the Beverley firm of solicitors, Messrs Crust Todd Mills and Co allowed us to consult documents in their keeping. We have further been assisted by many librarians and archivists, and to all we record our gratitude for their patience and helpfulness: to the British Library, the City Libraries of Hull and York, the Brynmor Jones Library at the University of Hull, and the Borough Library at Beverley. Among the archivists whom we would especially thank are those at the Public Record Office, Cumbria Record Office, Carlisle, the County Record Offices of Humberside and North Yorkshire, the manuscripts departments at the Universities of Hull and Nottingham, and the House of Lords Record Office.

Our text has been commented on by a number of scholars, and we would particularly thank Dr J. V. Beckett, University of Nottingham; Dr P. Roebuck, New University of Ulster; and Professor Norman Lewis, University of Sheffield. We are especially indebted to Mrs Eileen Spring and Professor F. M. L. Thompson, both of whom read a late draft.

Finally, the research on which this monograph was based was funded by the Social Science Research Council. We are much obliged to them for their generous assistance, as we are also to our own University for the excellent research facilities it offers its members.

BARBARA ENGLISH
JOHN SAVILLE

UNIVERSITY OF HULL
JANUARY 1983

CONTENTS

CHAPTER I THE MODEL

CHAPTER II REALITY

It was stated in the House of Commons by a king's counsel of considerable practice in the courts of common law, that there were not above six persons who understood the laws of real property, and it may be safely asserted that, with the exception of Mr Sugden, there is no barrister of eminence practising in any of the courts who has a perfect knowledge of their practical effects.

First Report of the Commissioners of Inquiry into the Law of England respecting Real Property
PP 1829 (263) X 563

The desire of great landowners has constantly been to make the strictest settlements which the law would allow, and the law, as we shall immediately see, has set bounds, though liberal ones, to the power of fettering inheritances and suspending absolute ownership. And the ingenuity of conveyancers, devising how to satisfy private ambition to the utmost within the field left clear to it by public ordinance, has produced that curious and exquisite structure, which, a hundred years hence, may peradventure be as much abandoned to the care of a few legal antiquaries as the learning of disseisin and collateral warranty.

F. Pollock, *The Land Laws* (1883) 112–13

Chapter I The Model

1 Introductory

The squire of a great country house, in the eighteenth or nineteenth century, standing on his terrace looking out across his broad acres, was rarely the owner of his land or even his house. He was the life tenant, in possession of the family capital but unable to deal with his estates as if he owned them outright. His interests were subordinate to those of the family, and the family was of more importance than he was. He was the king in check, his freedom of manoeuvre limited by a peculiarly English system of inheritance, the strict settlement[1]. Most of the greater landowners of England, from the end of the seventeenth century to the end of the nineteenth century, held their land, or part of their land, under settlement. A settlement was the generic name for the whole transaction of arranging for the transmission of property; it was also used of the deed or set of deeds by which the succession to land was subject to limitations[2]. As practised in England, settlement was a mixture of a small amount of statute law and a large amount of tradition; it was not the result of any one statute, but rather an amalgamation of common law, equity and conveyancing devices, tested in the courts over the years, and subject to periodic refinement by legal decision or statute. The particular mix of statute and tradition differed at different periods. The legal processes involved are complex, and both land reformers and historians have at times over-simplified the way in which settlements were actually constructed, and, having arrived at a simplified model, drawn deductions from it which have been misleading.

We do not propose, at present, to debate the historical consequences of settlement; and at this stage we are making no statement about the connection of settlements with some of their real or alleged economic results, such as the rise of great estates, effects on the land market, aristocratic indebtedness, under-capitalisation of agricultural improvements, or the position of heiresses and younger children. We wish only to explore the variety of settlement as practised over two and a half centuries; the particular occasions on which landowning families settled their estates; and the pattern of settlement in families from about 1660 until the beginning of the twentieth century. This period is a long one, but although the details of settlements became more complicated over the two and a half centuries, as the decisions of courts and changing circumstances led to the inclusion of additional clauses, their basic structure remained unchanged from Bridgeman's precedents of the late seventeenth century to Davidson's precedents of 1880[3].

What we are attempting here is first, the construction of a model of strict settlement, and then, in the chapter which follows, a demonstration of the variety of experience in family settlement over time and in different parts of the country on different estates. The selection of families has to some extent been dictated by the availability of material. This leads to the consequence that the families whose settlements are investigated over the whole of the two centuries tend to be those that were successful in maintaining their status, those that survived into the twentieth century in sufficient style to keep their archives. It is not difficult to find the settlement deeds of the dukes of Bedford: it would be very difficult, perhaps impossible, to trace those of all the landed families whose downfall is recorded in such works as Burke's *Vicissitudes of Families*[4]. There are, however, some examples of families that suffered financial disaster, such as the Herons of Chipchase, the Verneys of Claydon, the Myddeltons of Chirk and the dukes of Buckingham. Only financial disaster, it should be noted, could cause a landed family to fail, that is, lose all its land: in the case of a lack of direct heirs, there was always someone who would inherit, either under a settlement, or, if there was no settlement, as heir at law under common law rules.

An attempt has also been made in this general survey to balance the great landowners with lesser landowners and squires. Even single farms, it may be noted, could be strictly settled: the East Riding provided at least two examples, one in the eighteenth and one in the nineteenth century[5].

2 Origins and history of strict settlement

There were several different kinds of settlement[6], but the kind used by the great landowners acquired its descriptive label 'strict' (=restricted) because it was restricted to certain named successors and 'the heirs of their body lawfully begotten'[7]. Neither the word 'settlement' nor the term 'strict' needed to be included in the documents that set up a family settlement; the transactions were recognisable by what they executed, rather than by the type of conveyance, and indeed many varying types of conveyances were used, including wills[8]. Settlements also differed in the extent to which they curbed the life tenant.

Three elements from different centuries came together to make the structure of the strict settlement. When these three had been combined in conveyances, tested and accepted by the courts during the latter part of the seventeenth century, there were still some aspects of settlement which remained to be clarified (such as the exact way in which the length of time that a settlement could last was calculated) and these were determined by legislative changes or judicial decisions of the eighteenth and early nineteenth centuries. But by 1700 the framework of settlement was substantially complete. The three elements which, through the ingenuity of conveyancers, made what Pollock described as 'that curious and exquisite structure'[9] were the fee tail (or entail) assured by the statute *De Donis Conditionalibus* (1285); the life interest which could be created under the Statute of Uses (1535); and the seventeenth-century device of 'trustees to preserve the contingent remainders'[10].

De Donis Conditionalibus (that is 'concerning conditional gifts') were the operative words of Edward I's Statute of Westminster II, which protected those grants made to a man and the heirs of his body (or, most commonly, heirs male of his body). In a grant of this kind, the descent of the land was cut down, restricted to a particular line of succession, which was called in law 'feodum talliatum', or cut down fee, generally referred to as an estate tail or entail. From the time of the statute of 1285, an existing entail was enforceable at law, and unless the entail could somehow be destroyed, entailed land passed to the lineal successor of the grantee for generation after generation, as long as there were heirs of the prescribed class.

The protection of entails, thus established in 1285, lasted for some 200 years. In the fifteenth century, although the Statute of Westminster II still remained in force, a legal device, the 'common recovery', became accepted in the courts as a means of barring an entail. The basis of the common recovery was a fictitious law suit, in which a third party was asked to guarantee a title to a freehold: when the third party (it became customary to use the court crier) defaulted and did not offer any guarantee, the land was freed of its incumbrances (in this case the entail) and granted to the plaintiff, who then by pre-arrangement reconveyed the land to the defendant. The common recovery continued to evolve in complexity and was the usual way of barring an entail until 1833, when it was abolished and a simpler disentailing assurance substituted. It was also possible to use another collusive action ending in a final concord or 'fine', but that only allowed a partial freeing of the entail.

From the fifteenth century, for about 200 years, entails were easily broken, and the courts rejected attempts by lawyers to establish more permanent settlements. The device of the common recovery allowed the tenant in tail in possession of the land to break the entail: the efforts of the lawyers were therefore directed towards ensuring that there was never a tenant in tail in possession of the land but only a series of life tenants; before the tenant in tail could inherit, he was persuaded to resettle in such a way as to become himself a life tenant, with another, remoter, tenant in tail in a future generation. The key to this development was the concept of the life tenancy. By the early seventeenth century some families, in certain counties at least, were settling all or the greater part of their estates by giving successive life interests to the landowner and to his eldest son, designating the son's unborn eldest son tenant in tail[11].

The statute that was the basis of the life tenancy was the Statute of Uses (1535), a statute which remained the legal (as opposed to equitable) basis of settlements until the Settled Land Act of 1925. The 1535 statute was an attempt by the Government to claw back for the Crown fiscal advantages which had been disappearing through the proliferation of 'uses'. Before the Statute of Uses, if A conveyed land to B for the use of C, C had the benefit and profit, but B remained the legal owner. After the statute, the man with the benefit or 'use' (C in the example) had the 'legal estate', approximately the same as ownership. The simplest form of settlement granted land to one or more persons and their heirs for the use of (naming the first life tenant) for his life. The Statute of Uses then operated to turn the man with the use into the possessor of the legal estate: but only for his life, not absolutely.

The period between the Statute of Uses and the Civil War was one of great confusion in conveyancing, with a great diversity of practice and much overturning of earlier judicial decisions by later judges. The two elements of the future strict settlement already in existence were the fee tail and the life tenancy or life interest: the point at which a settlement based on these two kept breaking down was the problem of 'contingent remainders'. Land could be granted to a person for his life and entailed after his death on his existing children[12]. But if the property was left in remainder to an unborn person, that remainder could only be contingent, because that person might never be born and so the remainder might never happen: it might never 'vest' was the technical term. If the remainder was contingent only, the life tenant might safely destroy it. Although the destruction of the remainder was a wrongful act, it was not against the common law (it could be effected legally by the common recovery) nor did it come into the Chancellor's equitable jurisdiction because there was no breach of trust.

The problem of the contingent remainders was solved by including trustees in the settlement, whose trust became operative whenever there were contingent remainders to protect. The troubles of the mid seventeenth century produced this device and several other conveyancing expedients to preserve landed estates: and in addition to these, the abolition of military tenures by the Restoration Parliament meant that after 1660 land could be freely devised (and therefore settled) by will. From about 1660, therefore, settlements made by the living or settlements made by will to take effect on death became more common and more effective, and they contained clauses which were evolving towards the comprehensive strict settlements of the nineteenth century, built around the entail, the life tenancy, and the trustees to preserve the contingent remainders.

The idea of using trustees to preserve contingent remainders in family settlements is usually credited to Orlando Bridgeman (or Bridgman) (1606?–1674), in association with Geoffrey Palmer (1598–1670). Bridgeman was a leading lawyer of the mid seventeenth century, who took to conveyancing during the Commonwealth because his royalist politics kept him out of public office. It has been shown, however, that Bridgeman did not always include the clause in his drafts, and did not use it in his own family's settlements until 1670[13]. Bridgeman's settlements, in fact, showed little regularity in their phrases, and it is difficult to be sure if they were what later generations would call strict settlements or not; for instance, one of Bridgeman's settlements that can be dated from internal evidence to 1641–2 (relating to the earl of Northumberland) entailed the estates, established a series of life tenancies, was restricted and had trustees to protect remainders; but the trustees were used to protect the minorities of successors in being, and not unborn successors[14]. Strict settlement, it must be again emphasised, was the result of evolution as well as invention. However, as early as 1675, Francis North, who like Bridgeman was ultimately Lord Keeper, rewrote the draft of his father's settlement contained in his will, because the settlement did not have trustees to support the contingent remainders to unborn children, and could therefore easily be over-turned[15]. It would seem that between about 1650 and 1675 leading lawyers had come to expect the contingent remainders to be safeguarded. Nevertheless, eighteenth-century definitions of strict settlement concentrated on the restrictions of the entail and not on the contingent remainders: while it is hardly definitive proof, it may be noted that it was only in 1841 that the trustees were included in the definitions cited by the *OED*[16].

One further essential attribute of the strict settlement was worked out in the later seventeeth century and succeeding decades; the courts gradually established the length of time that a settlement of land could last. The law 'abhorred a perpetuity' (this was a maxim and not a statutory provision) and while great landowners seem to have wanted perpetual entails, the courts at most times tried to restrict them. Seventeenth-century decisions left it uncertain whether or not settlement could include unborn successors; in 1736 the length of time a settlement could last was fixed as a life or lives in being plus 21 years, and finally, in the House of Lords' ruling in *Cadell* v. *Palmer* (1833), the rule against perpetuities reached its modern form[17]. The rule against perpetuities was one of the few principles that affected settlements; others were that conditions imposed by settlements must be reasonable, or Chancery might overturn the settlement; the Statute of Enrollments; the Statute of Frauds; and (from 1800) Thellusson's Act which prohibited long-term accumulation of income under a settlement.

The strict settlement was used by landowners from the later seventeenth century into the twentieth century, finally becoming obsolete for reasons that were mainly fiscal. By the end of the nineteenth century it was changing in character, although it still dominated the inheritance patterns of most landed estates. Successive statutes of the nineteenth century (see below, p.51) had strengthened the powers of the life tenant, and after the Settled Land Act of 1882 settlements were no longer concerned with a specific estate, or with a particular group of lands, but with the capital that the estate or lands represented. After 1882 the life tenant could, if he wished, sell the family lands and reinvest the money in other land or in government funds: but whatever he did with the capital, it was still not his outright, but continued to be governed by the trusts of the settlement and thereby protected by the trustees. For example, if the settled lands had been charged with a payment of £1000 a year to the life tenant's widowed mother, and entailed after his death on his son, the life tenant could sell the settled lands, but whatever he received in return for the lands was still charged with the annual payment and was still entailed on his son[18].

3 The basic structure

Every record office contains dozens of family settlements. In the whole country there are thousands, made by deed in the lifetime of the owners, or by will to take effect at death. The law reports are a prolific source of information about settlements: Sugden, writing in 1861 on powers created by settlement, cited approximately 2500 separate cases in which some part of a settlement had been at issue[19]. The records of Parliament contain many hundreds of private estate acts, passed in order to modify family settlements, which contained clear statements about the individual arrangements made. A large proportion of the work of the House of Lords was concerned with appeals and the great majority of the appeal cases concerned the ownership of land, generally arising as the result of a complex family settlement[20]. The death duty registers now available in the Public Record Office, covering the years 1796 to 1903, contain abstracts of hundreds of settlements which governed the tenure and descent of great estates. Even plays, novels, literary anecdotes, and paintings portrayed elements of settlements[21]. There was also a long series of printed precedent books, volumes compiled to provide conveyancers with outlines of deeds, which included precedents of settlements[22]. From all this material it is possible to reconstruct the features of a typical settlement (below, pp.19–21).

Settlements were like leaves on a tree: all different, yet nevertheless recognisably leaves of the same tree. A settlement could be made to do anything: 'there is no event, or combination of events, which can possibly happen in a family, of whatever rank or number, but what may be provided for and met, by a family settlement framed by a master of his art.'[23] The making of settlements was, however, not an easy skill to acquire, nor are settlements easy documents to understand. English real property law (of which settlements were a signficant part) grew in complexity over the years until, in 1826, on the eve of the conveyancing reforms of the nineteenth century, a lawyer could say that to study the laws of real property he needed a working library of 674 volumes, exclusive of indices to the statutes[24].

From the historian's point of view, settlement deeds were very long and full of repetition. Until the Conveyancing Act of 1881, solicitors were paid for conveyances by the word (1*s* for every 72 words in 1862), a method of remuneration which did not encourage conciseness[25]. Part of a family settlement of the estates of the marquis of Hertford made in 1802 (the deed of release) comprised 77 sheets of parchment[26], and the Sykes settlement of midsummer 1847 consisted of six separate deeds[27]. The lines of writing might be more than two feet long: the habit of not punctuating a deed made it difficult to find a resting place for the eye while reading, a criticism which Jeremy Bentham made[28]. 'If you attempt to read one', complained Joshua Williams, the leading property lawyer of the mid nineteenth century, 'you must keep the finger of one hand at one end of the line, to see where you left off, and the other at the other end to find out where you are to begin again.'[29]

But in practice only a small part of the deed contained new information, and most of it consisted of common form phrases which were once necessary to comply with legal requirements, but which do not add to the historian's knowledge. The new information was usually signalled in the deed by a phrase in capital letters: for instance, a deed which opened with a long recital of previous transactions to prove a good title, at the point when the recital had ended and the current conveyance was about to be described, would contain the words, 'NOW THIS INDENTURE WITNESSETH'. By looking at the new information only, it is possible to analyse a settlement deed (or, of course, any other deed) into a number of different clauses or sets of clauses. These clauses were similar in all settlements (whether made in the settlor's lifetime or to take effect by his will), although they might be arranged in varying order: wills in particular showed a great variety of form. An outline of the usual elements of a settlement is given below. The whole range of clauses is that which might appear in a fully-developed nineteenth-century settlement deed of about 1840. The late seventeenth-century deed of settlement was shorter and much less complex, because the structure was not yet fully evolved, and the later nineteenth-century deed was also shorter and less complex, for nineteenth-century legal reform, partial as it was, led to some clauses being taken for granted (and therefore omitted).

The clauses of a settlement deed of the mid nineteenth century were commonly as follows:

The Premises set out the date and the names and occupation or rank of the parties, that is, the settlor and those adults involved in the settlement, including the trustees (and there could be several different sets of trustees involved).

The Recitals of previous transactions relating to the present deed showed the title to the property and any incumbrances on it, usually consisting of many sentences beginning WHEREAS.

The Testatum set out the purpose of the deed. This, marked by the word WITNESSETH, gave (a) the consideration on which the settlement was made (usually on the ground of 'natural love and affection' or in connection with marriage: 'consideration' did not apply in wills); (b) the intention of the deed; (c) the description of the property to be settled, known as 'the parcels', introduced by the phrase ALL THAT, often described generally in this part of the deed and more specifically in a schedule at the end; (d) any exceptions to the property to be settled.

The Habendum contained the main trusts of the deed, signalled by the words TO HAVE AND TO HOLD. The first trusts were those that related to the settlor. All the subsidiary trusts were then described and the property was conveyed to the trustees for terms of years or in fee. The subsidiary trusts were likely to be all or some of the list which follows: (a) an annuity to the heir until he succeeded (considered further below); (b) pin-money (that is, pocket money during marriage) to the settlor's wife, and his heir's wife, if he were married; (c) jointures (that is, money after the husband's death) to the settlor's widow, and his heir's widow; and (d) portions (capital sums) to the younger children of the settlor and of the heir, if any. All trusts contained clauses about the operation of the trusts, and what the trustees and beneficiaries might or might not do. The subsidiary trusts were put near the beginning of the settlement deed, and before the establishment of the entail, so that the subsidiary trusts could not be over-turned when the entail was at some future time barred (i.e. destroyed) by a tenant in tail.

The Entail set out the order of succession of life tenants, and created a life estate or series of life estates for persons already born, and after that a series of fee tail estates for persons yet unborn. The entail is considered further below. A term of years or sometimes the fee simple would be granted to trustees to preserve any contingent remainders. This section of the deed could specify conditions of inheritance, such as that an inheritor should take the name and arms of the settlor, or (if he refused) be passed over in the succession; and it sometimes included a clause (a 'shifting use') that if the heir inherited another estate he should pass on the estate, now being settled on him, to the next heir[30]. After the entail had been set out, there was an ultimate remainder, usually to the settlor and his heirs.

The Powers. There followed the powers granted to the trustees and the life tenants, either acting separately or together. These could be of many kinds. The trustees and/or life tenants were granted power to charge the estates with (a) pin-money; (b) jointures and (c) portions. They could also be granted power (d) to make leases (ordinary, building, repairing, mining and quarrying); (e) to grant licences to copyholders and to enfranchise copyholds: (f) to deal with leasehold land by renewing the leases and performing the covenants of the leases; and (g) to sell, exchange and/or mortgage settled land for certain purposes (the money or land thus acquired remaining to the uses of the settlement). Finally there might be (h) a general power of appointment, which was a clause allowing the life tenant a considerable measure of freedom. All these powers are considered in more detail below.

Heirlooms. Great landowners often designated certain of the contents of their family mansions as heirlooms, and directed that they were to stay with the successive life tenants.

Trustees. A number of clauses enabled the trustees (a) to give valid receipts; (b) to appoint new trustees (sometimes this was left to the life tenant); (c) to be indemnified against certain claims; and (d) to be reimbursed for their expenses.

Testimonium. The last and formal clauses, introduced by the words IN WITNESS WHEREOF, declared that the parties had signed and sealed the deed before witnesses.

Certain of the clauses of a family settlement as set out above are more difficult to decode than others; inevitably some are of more interest to historians than others. Although the premises, recitals, *testatum* and *testimonium* clauses contain essential information, they are easily understood; but certain of the more complex aspects of the settlement deeds are now further discussed.

(i) *Annuity to the heir.* The first trust to be included in a settlement was usually the grant of an annuity to the heir until he succeeded to the estates. The heir was not likely to have been granted the right to such an annuity under any previous family settlements (unlike his younger brothers and sisters, whose annuities and portions are dealt with under powers, below, pp.26–7), for the lack of an independent income was one of the levers which persuaded the heir to agree to resettle the estates when he came of age.

The heir who was tenant in tail was, theoretically, but only theoretically, in a strong position when he came of age at 21. If he refused to co-operate with his father (or other life tenant, perhaps his grandfather, uncle or cousin)[31], the entail could not be broken, and the tenant in tail must eventually inherit lands that he could easily turn into a fee simple. The difficulty was to survive in the meantime: until he succeeded to the estate, at a time which might be years away, he would have to live on his expectations and his wits, for it was traditional that even if a sum had been assigned to the younger children in a previous settlement, it would not include the heir. He could try to borrow on his life interest, as the poet Shelley tried, unsuccessfully[32]; he could sell his own expectation and that of his own direct descendants, as Thomas Transome in George Eliot's novel *Felix Holt* had done: but such a 'base fee' as it was called, was an insecure title, for it depended on the survival of the direct line of the seller and therefore was not worth very much. In practice the prospect of an immediate income, possibly with future increments, which would allow him to set up an establishment of his own, as well as the strong pressures of family tradition, persuaded the tenant in tail to join the life tenant in resettling. A well-known solicitor declared in 1881 that he had never known a son to refuse[33].

(ii) *The entail.* The dominant feature of the settlement was the pattern of succession it established: the entail. A simple form of entail might be included in a deed made by a landowner, reserving a life estate for himself, after his death leaving his land to his eldest son for life, with remainder to his eldest son's son in fee tail, and remainders to other members of the family, should the first line fail, each stage being protected by trustees. In fact family settlements were considerably more complex than this simple model. Apart from making arrangements for the immediate and obvious heirs, the settlement would set out remainders to more distant heirs. A precedent book of 1833[34] giving a form for establishing a strict settlement before marriage, settled the land in remainder to the first son of the marriage and the heirs male of the body of such first son: and for default of such issue, then to the use of the 2nd, 3rd, 4th and all and every other son and sons 'severally, successively and in remainder, one after another, as they shall be in seniority of age and priority of birth, and of the several and respective heirs male of the body and bodies of all and every such son and sons, the elder of such sons and heirs male of his body always to be preferred and to take before the younger of such sons and the heirs male of his and their body and bodies' (this way of setting out the succession was more conveniently described as 'in tail male'). The arrangements for the sons in tail male were followed by similar clauses for the sons in tail general (clauses that let in the whole line of the sons' descendants, male and female); then there were successive remainders to the daughters in common (sharing equally) and in tail general. It is common to find families who favoured tail male through many generations over tail general: that is, they would allow distant male relatives to succeed before much more closely related females. Other remainders to people outside the immediate family could follow and in the greater landowning families there might be many potential life tenants and their male children named in a settlement reaching as far as remote cousins. It was common, although not an invariable rule, to give living persons a life tenancy only; unborn successors could not be named as life tenants, but had to be tenants in tail. Examples of complex entails, mixing life tenancies and tenancies in tail are given below (Ch.II). The entail would end with an ultimate remainder to the 'right heirs', that is, in the event of the named successors and their lines dying out, the common law rules of inheritance would be applied and the courts would decide who had the best right to inherit.

No part of the settlement could be broken (except by act of Parliament) until a person named in the entail as tenant in tail came of age; then, joining with his father or other life tenant (or acting alone if he was already in possession of the estates) the entail could be ended, by the legal processes of 'suffering a common recovery' or by 'levying a fine'. Once the entail was broken, all parts of the deed of settlement subsequent to the clauses relating to the entail were also void. What happened next depended on the parties, but the usual practice was that a new strict settlement was made, with the former life tenant being made life tenant once more, his son also being named as a future life tenant after him, and his son's son tenant in tail. This process might and often did continue for generations.

Provisions for widows and younger children, power to lease and mortgage, were also usually written into the deeds (and if such powers were not specifically granted, they could not be exercised), but the main purpose of settlement was to set out the succession to the estates and to prevent the man in possession of the land alienating it. It was, of course, legally possible to name any person in a settlement; it was custom that kept it to near relatives, and custom that emphasised primogeniture. Horace Walpole claimed that it was usual to establish entails on the 'nearest of blood' and 'very unusual and uncommonly generous to place in the room of such near relations others more distant . . .'[35].

If a man died without making any arrangements for the inheritance of his property – that is, intestate – by English law the eldest son succeeded to everything, to the exclusion of the younger children and even of the widow. If there were no son, the real estate was divided equally among the daughters. The principle as well as the effects of the *law* of primogeniture were much attacked by nineteenth-century reformers: but it was very rare for great landowners to die without having made a will or some arrangement for the succession to their property, so that the law was rarely invoked in their case[36]. The *custom* of primogeniture, however, was so strong in the landowning classes that English aristocrats and English squires overwhelmingly favoured their eldest sons in their arrangements for the future; among peers and baronets this ensured that the family land stayed with the title. Even when the government passed the notorious penal law against Irish Catholic landowners in 1704, which allowed only a Protestant eldest son to succeed to the whole estate (Catholic sons must take equal shares) primogeniture survived to this extent, that the government would not put a Protestant younger son in the place of a Catholic heir and give him everything[37]. In Trumbach's study of settlement in thirty English families in the eighteenth century, only once was an eldest son disinherited[38]; in the case histories below (chapter II), the eldest son almost invariably succeeded[39]. If a man had no sons, he might, however, choose a younger son from another branch of the family to make his heir, so that two estates would not merge.

Normally a man without sons would settle his estates on a near male relative of an appropriate generation. Male relatives were favoured over females: Dr Johnson's view was shared by many landowners 'an ancient estate should always go to males. It is mighty foolish to let a stranger have it because he marries your daughter and takes your name'[40].

4 Powers

The group of clauses which allowed an infinite variety in settlement, which gave flexibility to it and made it workable, were collectively called powers. Powers developed from the sixteenth century onwards[41] and were used in settlements to provide for wives and younger children and for the management of the estates to the best advantage by authorising leases, sales, exchanges or mortgages. Normally, powers were included in settlements to provide the following:

(i) *Pin-money*. This was an annual allowance made for a wife during her husband's lifetime, under a trust, and assured by powers of distress and entry. Until the first Married Women's Property Act of 1870, trustees had to be involved, since a wife could not own anything herself. Pin-money as a phrase occurs first in the sixteenth century[42]; the object was to provide the wife with a dress allowance and pocket money for charities and for gifts[43]. She could do what she liked with it: she could save it up and leave it to someone in her will, or give it away in her lifetime. She could not, however, anticipate it; and she could not get more than one year's arrears after her husband's death. The amount of pin-money was not very large: there were other ways of making wives financially independent of their husbands, by establishing separate trusts for them. An 1833 precedent gave a wife who brought to the marriage a fortune of £12,000 in 3% Consols £200 a year pin-money[44].

(ii) *Jointure*. If a woman married to a life tenant survived her husband, she was almost invariably entitled under the marriage settlement to an annual sum, a jointure, paid to her. Jointures were often an annual percentage return on the fortune (or dowry) the wife brought to the marriage. Many examples of the ratio of jointure to fortune are in print, because it is a topic of much interest to economic historians[45]. Ratios of 5 per cent to 20 per cent occurred, but around

10 per cent seemed the commonest figure. In the case of a family practising strict settlement, if the jointure was to be charged on the land (and not paid out of income, which would be less acceptable to the bride's family, as it was not so certain) power to charge jointure at a certain percentage of the wife's fortune, and/or up to a certain ceiling, was included in the settlement, made perhaps long before the marriage was considered. Often the girl's fortune had also been fixed years before by the settlement in her family, so that the matching of the fortune of the bride to the maximum allowed in the bridegroom's existing family settlement was critical. Such calculations did not apply when the bride was an heiress, with her fortune in land, because her land could be settled separately on her and therefore support her as a widow.

Jointures were sometimes increased at resettlements, or even by private act of Parliament. They were paid whether or not the widow married again, but, of course, in any event for her life only. As with pin-money, powers of distress and entry enabled the widow to be sure of her annuity, which had to be paid at specified times and places. Sometimes designated parts of the estate (trust estates) paid the charge, not the whole estate[46]. Sometimes, instead of or as well as money, property was settled on the lady should she become a widow; the dower house was a feature of English country life, and a detached estate might provide a comfortable old age for the life tenant's widow (the dowager) while the next life tenant inherited the family mansion[47].

(iii) *Portions*. These were included in settlements as regularly as jointures. They were provisions made for younger children of the life tenants. Before the eighteenth century younger sons were often given annuities – later both sexes were usually treated alike[48]. Portions were sums of capital paid to the younger children on attaining their majority, or on marriage, provided out of the rents and profits of the estate, or by mortgage on part or all of the estate, or by sale of part of the estates. They were usually raised at the father's death, or in life at his request[49]. Without the power of portioning his future daughters, a man could find it difficult to make a suitable marriage[50]. Eldest sons were not given portions or annuities until resettlement, for reasons shown above (pp.21–2).

Settlements often included clauses to allow anticipation of the portions, to keep and educate the children while under age, and possibly to advance their careers: for instance, to buy a son a service commission, or put him into a profession. Sometimes only a certain percentage of the total was allowed for maintenance: 4 per cent seems to have been usual. Portions were not always paid even when due, and in this case interest might be paid instead[51] but if the portion was due, and the recipient needed it, he could assign his interest to someone else, in return for the money.

Like jointures, portions have been of interest to historians as affecting the economy of estates, and many examples of portions, and discussion of their effects, are in print[52]. Portions, even more often than jointures, were specified in advance of the event: in this case, in advance of the birth of the children who would benefit. It was customary to make a sliding scale for children, related to the annual rental, with a fixed maximum. Sometimes the settlement laid down that the portion fund was to be divided equally; sometimes a power of appointment was given to the life tenant to divide the portion money as he thought fit among the younger children, it being understood that if the power was not used, the portion fund was divided equally. The power to appoint among the children gave the parents some influence over the children's behaviour and especially over their marriage; for one child could be given nearly everything, and another be 'cut off with a shilling'[53]. Usually clauses relating to portion money included a 'hotchpot' clause; if any child's portion was advanced, before the general distribution, the amount of the advance was to be taken into account. Suppose a man had five younger children, and a provision of £50,000 for portions, out of which he gave one child £10,000 on marriage, but did not use his power of appointment again before he died: it was possible (without the hotchpot clause) that the child with the £10,000 would then also take a fifth of the remaining £40,000[54].

(iv) *Leases*. If a man was a tenant for life, without a specific power of leasing, he could not grant a lease beyond his own life[55]. It was, however, customary to include in a strict settlement a power to make leases, usually for 21 years for ordinary (agricultural) purposes and for longer, perhaps 99 years, for building leases, or for 40 or 60 years for repairing, mining and quarrying leases. Many powers of leasing restrained the lessor from taking any fine on granting a lease. A fine was a sum which might be paid by the tenant on taking a lease, which could be used to decrease his rent, and therefore the life tenant (because he could keep the fine) benefitted at the expense of his successor (who might inherit a binding lease at an uneconomic rent). If an entry fine was accepted when specifically prohibited by the settlement, the life tenant had committed a fraud on the power, and the lease would be void. The life tenant was also to take the best rent he could get: not necessarily the highest offer, for he was entitled to consider the character of the tenant[56]. A rent of the full annual value of the tenement, a rack-rent, was sometimes specified. Leases might contain 'the usual covenants' which were not about agricultural affairs, but about the process in the event of non-payment of rents, and keeping the premises in repair[57]. The whole question of leases, if they were tightly controlled by the settlement, was of great importance in the development of the estates. Wide powers of leasing were usually included: much of London was built on land leased for 99 years[58].

(v) *Waste.* In most family settlements there was a clause allowing the life tenant of the settlement to be 'without impeachment of waste', that is, he was not liable for certain kinds of damage he might do to the property. The basis of the rule about waste was that a successor's rights must be protected, and in certain circumstances, the removal of trees, hedges, parts of or whole buildings, or opening new mines, quarries or peat bogs, was waste. In its most extreme form it could be called waste to turn arable lands into pasture or pasture into arable[59]. The life tenant was usually permitted waste of most kinds: the agricultural lessee of the life tenant usually not, and a clause of this kind was normally strictly interpreted.

(vi) *Copyhold and leasehold.* Further powers enabled the life tenants and/or trustees to deal with copyhold and leasehold property in the same way as freehold, including the power (after 1853) to enfranchise, i.e. convert copyholds into freeholds. Many large estates held areas of copyhold land (held under a title of a copy of the manor court roll) and leasehold (often leased from a corporate body such as a college or the church)[60].

(vii) *Sale, mortgage, exchange.* Powers could be included in settlements to allow the trustees, with the consent of the life tenant or at their discretion if the life tenant was under age, to sell, mortgage or exchange parts of the settled estates, with the condition that the money raised could only be used to redeem incumbrances on the lands, or to reinvest in land which was to be settled in accordance with the terms of the original settlement. Often it was specified that the land had to be in England or Wales, thus avoiding both risky speculations in Irish acres and the complexity of the Scottish succession laws. The principal mansion house and its park were usually excluded from these powers. It was in some settlements possible to exchange some of the landowner's free lands for settled lands, by conveying the free lands to the uses of the settlement and then abstracting from the settlement lands of the same value. It was customary in settlements made by will to allow the trustees to raise money by mortgage, if necessary, to add to the personal estate in order to pay the testator's debts and legacies. Powers of mortgaging for specific improvements (such as draining agricultural land, or extending the mansion) could also be granted.

Wide ranging powers of sale, exchange or mortgage were of great significance in the family settlement, for they allowed the life tenant a considerable degree of freedom from the restrictions of his settlement. According to Joshua Williams, they were 'usually inserted in settlements'[61] and this seems to have been the nineteenth-century position. Like all other powers, if they were not included in the settlement, or permitted by statute, the only way in which they could be obtained was by the life tenant acquiring a private act of Parliament. 'Statute' in the above context includes enclosure acts, dock and canal acts, and other acts for public utilities; these acts customarily included provisions to allow life tenants to sell, exchange or mortgage their estates.

(viii) *General power of appointment.* The final power considered is the oddly named 'general power of appointment'. Sometimes, towards the end of a deed, when a great number of detailed clauses had been set out, a clause would be included conveying some or all of the estates 'to such use or uses as the settlor [or the settlor and his heir] shall at any time, by deed or will made in the proper form direct limit and appoint, with or without power of revocation; and in default of such direction or appointment, to the use of the previously described settlement.'

The general power of appointment to new uses was known as early as the sixteenth century in the looser forms of settlement then available, but was the subject of judicial uncertainty in the seventeenth century and only became clarified in the eighteenth century[62]. The effect of such a clause was that the settlement continued to operate unless interfered with; but that at any time the possessor or possessors of the general power could revoke any or every part of the settlement, and make a new one if and as he pleased[63]. Settlements which contained this power transformed the deed of settlement into nothing more than a safety device, an umbrella under which the estates were protected from the hazard of the life tenant dying unexpectedly and leaving the estates unsettled. A general power of appointment conveyed on the man who could exercise the power the equivalent of absolute ownership. It allowed him, by exercising the power, to sell, exchange, lease or mortgage at will[64]. A general power of appointment could belong to the life tenant only; or to life tenant and prospective life tenant (who would usually be father and son) acting jointly; or other combinations, such as the life tenant and his brother. Sir Frederick Pollock wrote in the late nineteenth century that general powers were not usually included for they were 'inconsistent with the main object of making the estate as a whole as nearly inalienable as possible'[65]. Nevertheless they played an important part in the settlement history of great estates, even if they only operated for a short time. Examples are given in the case histories below (Ch.II).

5 The makers of settlements

Most of the great landowning families practised strict settlement, and they were imitated by gentry and even yeoman families. The amount of land in England held under settlement has never been established, and in any case the total must have varied from year to year, as family circumstances changed. Estimates made in the nineteenth century (earlier centuries did not record such speculations) varied from a quarter of all land to three quarters and upwards. As late as 1901 Sir Arthur Underhill, a conveyancing lawyer of great experience, wrote that 'nearly all the great estates, comprising perhaps the greater part of the land of England, are held in strict settlement'[66]. Professor F. M. L. Thompson thought that perhaps half the land of nineteenth-century England was in settlement[67]. The proportion remains unknown. Much calculation is required to find out how much land belonging to even one family was settled, and how much left out of settlement; how long an interval there was between settlements; or how strict the settlements were. Quantification of settled land in England is not at present (or perhaps ever) possible: we can only hope to offer impressions.

In the East Riding of Yorkshire, in 1875, eleven families each owned over 10,000 acres (between them, the eleven families owned 28 per cent of the Riding)[68]. The complete settlement history of all these families from 1660 to 1900 has not been traced. But there is sufficient evidence to show that strict settlement was practised by all but one of them at some time, although not by all the families continuously. Such evidence is to be found in the former East Riding Deeds Registry (now part of Humberside County Council Record Office) and the families' archives in public depositories, which contain either settlements, or abstracts of title referring to settlements. Private estate acts, chancery cases and the death duty registers also throw light on the families' settlements. It was the normal practice of these eleven families to make strict settlements, entailing their estates on their male heirs by deed or by will. Occasionally there were gaps between settlements by genealogical accident or because members of the family chose at a particular time to leave their land unsettled[69].

Settlements could be made by persons over the age of 21, provided they were not 'aliens, convicts, outlaws, bankrupts, insolvent, liquidating or compounding debtors, infants, lunatics, idiots or married women'[70]. Bankrupts and debtors could not make settlements, because that might defraud their creditors: lunatics and idiots could not make valid dispositions. But in all these cases (and in addition in some cases of outlawry and felony) an already existing settlement survived the disabilities of its life tenant, being administered by its trustees or sometimes by Chancery. Children under 21 years (legally known as infants) of either sex could not make binding settlements without a private act of Parliament, but many such acts were passed to enable young aristocrats to join in marriage settlements. After 1855, with the court's sanction, settlements of infants' estates could be made from the age of 20 for a boy and 17 for a girl[71].

An unmarried woman, who held a fee simple, could deal with her own property; but as soon as she married, and for as long as she remained married, she became legally incapable. At common law, a married woman was 'at an appalling proprietary disadvantage'[72]; during marriage, her husband had total power over her property, and if the couple had a child born alive, the husband's right remained for the rest of his life, even if he outlived his wife for many years. For in the view of the common law 'the husband and wife are one, and the husband is that one'[73]. In practice, however, the harshness of the common law was moderated by the doctrines of equity. The upper and middle classes did not wish their daughters to be entirely dependent on their husbands and sons, and they insisted on a marriage settlement for their womenfolk. A wife's property came to be protected by a trust, which took her property out of her husband's power and operated her 'separate estate' for her benefit. The trust was protected by the Court of Chancery. From the end of the eighteenth century the wife's separate estate was additionally protected from her own wish to alienate it or charge it, for many wives were put under pressure to allow their husband to deal with their property: it was supposed that the husband could 'kiss or kick' permission from his wife[74] and such compulsion was alleged by the duchess of Norfolk in 1700[75]. So that although equity would protect the wife's separate estate, from the late eighteenth century she was also prevented from settling it as she wished[76].

6 Occasions of settlement

Family settlements could be made at any time, and could affect the 100,000 acres of a duke or the 100-acre farm of a yeoman[77]. The most usual occasions for execution of a settlement were the coming of age of the heir, the marriage of the heir, or the death of the head of the family (under certain clauses of his will, which might have been made many years earlier, even in the year he succeeded to the estate).

If the land to be settled already lay under a strict settlement, then the first stage was to 'disentail', to terminate the old settlement, so that a new one could be made (see pp.14, 23 above).

(i) *The coming of age of the heir.* This was a ritual of great importance in the landed family. At 21 the young man had reached his legal majority: if he was tenant in tail of a family settlement, he was then able, together with his father, to break the entail and the family could take the opportunity of rearranging the estates and selling or mortgaging land, and making provision for other members of the family. Sometimes at the heir's majority the estates were immediately resettled: sometimes they were settled but subject to overriding powers known as general powers of appointment to be exercised by father and son for a long or short period, or the estates could be even left unsettled altogether. The freeing of the estates from the restrictions of settlement must have been eagerly awaited by some families, particularly those in financial difficulties. A settlement on the coming of age of the heir was delineated in Bridgeman's *Conveyances*[78]. In 1716 when the eldest son of John Liddell-Bright came of age, he joined with his father in disentailing his great-grandfather's settlement and the estates were strictly resettled[79]. When George, 3rd earl of Orford, came of age in 1751 as tenant in tail in possession, he disentailed the estates; and was then persuaded by his uncle, Horace Walpole senior, to agree to a 'mutual entail' whereby the Orford estates might pass to the Walpoles of Wolterton, and vice versa (an arrangement which overturned the settlement and entail originally made by Sir Robert Walpole, the 1st earl, and thus aroused the anger of Horace Walpole of Strawberry Hill). This mutual entail was made by the wills of both parties, about 1756, and would not come into effect until their deaths: during their lives only their sense of honour would prevent them altering the arrangements[80].

Sir Clifford Constable of Burton Constable in East Yorkshire became 21 in May 1827. His father had died, and as soon as he came of age, he was tenant in tail in possession. He began the process of disentailing, or rather his uncle and his lawyer did it for him, because Sir Clifford was travelling in Europe during the summer of 1827 and did not return until the autumn. Correspondence shows that the method of dealing with the estates was discussed between Sir Clifford's uncle, George Clifford, who was also his guardian and agent, and Iveson, his East Riding lawyer. The London conveyancer who was normally consulted by the family was also involved, as was the heir of the last surviving trustee of the existing settlement. Sir Clifford himself took little part: his uncle wrote that he listened to all the suggestions made 'in solemn silence' which his uncle took as consent, and the disentailing and resettlement deeds were taken over to Brussels for him to sign. The advisers discussed the advantages of leaving the estate as a fee simple, or alternatively resettling it at once. The East Yorkshire estates already had mortgages of £60,000 and additional sums had to be raised, of perhaps another £60,000. The easiest way to raise the money was on a fee simple, and George Clifford and the solicitor considered disentailing the estate and leaving it to be resettled at some future time, and protecting 'the chance of life' by Sir Clifford executing a will which in the event of his death could resettle the estate in the old way. Sir Clifford could then 'wait a further opportunity of his settling by Marriage or some other occasion'. The alternative plan to resettle at once seems to have been suggested because of Sir Clifford's spendthrift nature. At one stage George Clifford warned 'it will not be prudent to leave the fee simple and disposing power in Sir Clifford's hands for any, even a very short period of time' and that it would be better to write a resettlement into the disentailing deed so that there would be 'no interval of time between the expiration of the entail under Mr Constable's will and the commencement of the new one arising out of the new deed'. However a different plan was adopted, and the young heir broke the entail, and resettled strictly, but subject to a general power of appointment to be exercised by himself, which meant that he could do whatever he wanted with the estates. He then proceeded to mortgage them heavily[81].

A vivid picture of the events surrounding a resettlement comes from the archives of the Sykes family, of Sledmere in East Yorkshire. Although the resettlement is very late in the history of strict settlement (1900), it is quoted here as the best example the authors know of the kind of negotiation, usually unrecorded, that must have taken place many times on the heir's coming of age.

The background of the Sykes resettlement of 1900 was the mountain of debts of Lady Jessica, the estranged wife of Sir Tatton Sykes, 5th baronet. He had disclaimed her debts in 1896, and in 1897 there had been a court case over promissory notes signed by Lady Sykes. She was by 1896 borrowing money at a rate of 60 per cent annual interest; and by 1900 she owed, or disclosed, debts of £98,000. Mark Sykes, Tatton and Jessica's son, persuaded his father to agree to a resettlement on the eve of Mark's departure for the South African war and a first-hand account of this survives, in letters written by Mark to his future wife Edith Gorst[82].

Mark (who had long been involved in his parents' difficulties) asked for leave from the army, and spent March 1900 at Sledmere; he came of age on 6 March, and for the first time since 1847 disentailing and resettlement was possible. His father was reluctant to commit himself, but Mark persuaded him to agree to a letter embodying the outlines of an agreement. Sir Tatton promised to sign the letter the following day: so Mark left Sledmere arranging that Sir Tatton's agent would wire to Mark 'All right' and to the Beverley solicitor who acted for the family 'Yes'. But the following day Sir Tatton had 'lost' the letter, and his willingness to settle had evaporated. By April Mark was in despair, and had decided that his father was waiting for him to be killed in South Africa, so that no resettlement would have to be made. Eventually Mark told his father he was leaving for South Africa on 21 April, whether a settlement had been reached or not. The threat persuaded Sir Tatton to act.

On the evening of Friday 20 April, two sitting-rooms were engaged at the Hotel Metropole in London, where the elder Sykes usually stayed: in the first were Sir Tatton Sykes, his London solicitor, a head clerk and five other clerks, a conveyancing specialist, the Sledmere agent, and a solicitor for the Allied Assurance Company (the company was to lend £110,000); in the other room were Lady Jessica Sykes, two of her solicitors, and Mark's former tutor; accompanying Mark, as go-betweens, were his own solicitor, one of Jessica's solicitors and his two cousins. Negotiation lasted until early the next morning 'arguing, fighting, changing, erasing, quarrelling, cursing, go to-ing and fro-ing' from 9.45 p.m. until 1.00 a.m. By the morning of 21 April, when Mark left for South Africa, the resettlement was made: the estates had been disentailed and resettled once more, in the traditional manner but also including a mortgage of £110,000 to pay off Lady Jessica's debts.

(ii) *Marriage, particularly the marriage of the heir.* This was always a possible occasion for resettlement. In most cases marriage followed soon after majority[83], and the estates could therefore be disentailed on the heir's coming of age and left subject to a general power until he married. There was almost always a marriage settlement: no landed family liked its daughters to marry without one, since it could leave the bride at the mercy of an unscrupulous man or his family. Chancery always insisted on settlements for its wards[84]. In a large estate the marriage settlement might only settle part of the lands on the couple, with perhaps a subsidiary house: but a settlement there would be unless the marriage was a runaway one[85]. Marriage settlements could be pre-nuptial or post-nuptial; and sometimes the marriage took place on the basis of articles of agreement only, reached between the two families after much negotiation. The articles might in fact remain as the basis for a future settlement for years; if, in the meantime, one of the parties died, Chancery would enforce the execution of the articles[86]. In the 1690s, Sir Thomas Willoughby (later the 1st Lord Middleton) married under the aegis of articles of agreement, which were not converted into a marriage settlement until his first son was born some years later[87]. If a bride or bridegroom was under age when their marriage took place, it was possible to arrange their affairs temporarily by articles of agreement; but an act of Parliament was required to make an irrevocable settlement for a minor, so that when the duke of Rutland in 1717 wanted to marry his son to the daughter of Lord Lexinton he had to obtain a private act, for they were both under age[88].

Many family archives contain accounts of the making of a marriage settlement in the form of letters, diaries, memoirs or detailed solicitors' bills. The delicate business of matching the fortunes of bride and bridegroom was carried out by relatives, friends, lawyers, and even by marriage brokers until their activities were stopped by legal decisions[89]. In arranging marriages, the parties' social and economic status, their religion, character, appearance, age and affection for each other could all be considered. In different families and in different centuries these factors were of differing importance: some fathers might allow a choice to their children, so long as the choice was not 'impossible'[90]. The Blundell family of Crosby, Lancashire, kept a family memorandum suggesting alternative levels of settlement for brides of inferior or superior status[91] and some such considerations often came into the construction of a marriage settlement.

The negotiations of a marriage settlement required great tact and discretion. Both sides exchanged general information about their fortunes and expectations: when George Trevelyan was negotiating his marriage to Sir Walter Calverley's daughter in 1733, he supplied his prospective father-in-law with a memorandum of this kind:

> Sir, – I take my father's entailed estate to be £3,000 per annum; his acquired estate, £1,000 per annum. The estate he yields up to me immediately, to be £1,300 per annum . . . . The lady's jointure (called by the name of Lea Hill) is £1,060 per annum . . . .[92]

After a preliminary exchange of information, a detailed statement was then provided by the bride's solicitor for the bridegroom's solicitor containing the property to be settled on both sides, the provisions and the names of trustees proposed by the bridegroom's side leaving a blank for trustees proposed by the other side (the general rule being that an equal number should be nominated by each side). Pin-money, jointures and portions were the principal concern of the bride's solicitors in a strict settlement. The clients complained that the lawyers made it all very difficult; the lawyers complained that 'the clients are generally so ignorant of the nature of a settlement that they are unable to see the objects which their advisers are aiming at.'[93]

Much has been written about marriage settlements and the rise of the great estates, and there is no doubt about their importance. It needs to be emphasised, however, that whatever the contribution of marriage settlements to the enlargement of estates, they were only occasionally used to settle the whole of the family estates. Some settlement at marriage was nearly always made, but many marriage settlements were within the wider pattern of existing family settlements. What proportion of marriage settlements is to be equated with the strict settlement of either the total or a large part of estates, is not known; but it is less than is often assumed. The matter is further discussed below (pp.102–3, 114–15).

(iii) *Estates settled by will.* It was the practice of some landowners on entering estates, which were for some reason unsettled, to make wills to deal with the succession immediately, so that the land would not be inherited by the laws governing intestacy. Such wills must have often been replaced by subsequent settlements (and therefore been rendered obsolete), but they acted in the meantime as a safety device. For while settlements made on other occasions were irreversible (unless they contained general powers of revocation and new appointment) settlements made by will did not become operative until the testator died, so that throughout his life he was able to change his mind, destroy his existing will and make different arrangements. On quarrelling with his wife in 1686, the duke of Newcastle 'burnt his will and made another settlement'[94]. Nicholas Blundell of Crosby made six successive wills at the beginning of the eighteenth century, altering them as his family situation altered[95]. Sir James Lowther of Whitehaven made at least three wills (three have survived) relating to the settlement of his estates (see below, pp.74–5). Some wills were made long before they came into effect: the wills by which two men of the Downing family settled their estates in the late seventeenth and eighteenth centuries were made twenty-three and thirty-two years before death (see below, pp.68–71). The will of the earl of Orford in 1752, which settled his estates, was replaced by a will of 1756, but a codicil of 1776 restored the 1752 will and entail[96]. In a case of 1807 it was stated that the attorney instructed to make a settlement recommended a will rather than any other type of deed to his client, because it could be revoked or altered by codicil[97]. In the Fitzwilliam family, the elderly heir made a draft will in 1827 because of the age of his father, and the risk that the heir might die so soon after his father that he might not have the opportunity of making a will which, because of the great amount of property involved, would take some time[98]. Wills, because they were less formal than deeds, and were often made in haste and secrecy, caused far more problems to real estate lawyers than any other class of title deed[99].

Testators could use their wills to exercise any powers that had been granted to them in previous settlements. Parents, for instance, could use their wills to divide a portion fund between their younger children, dividing a previously established total sum in such ways as they chose; even, according to the catch phrase, cutting a child off with a shilling. Sometimes a will could make more drastic alterations: it could overturn a previous settlement, provided there were provisions for the settlor to use a general power of revocation and new appointment. Such a situation is illustrated in the will of Sir John Lowther of Whitehaven (see below, p.74). But without a general power, a tenant for life under a strict settlement could not alter the settlement by his will. He could, however, try to influence his successors, either by moral persuasion, or by the conditional bequest of his personal fortune, urging them to resettle according to his wishes when the opportunity should come. Examples of such persuasion can be seen in the settlement history of both the Hotham and Lowther familes (see below, pp.67, 74–5).

There are few records of the making of wills devising large landed estates outside fiction. Until the Wills Act of 1837, property acquired after the will was made could not be disposed of by any phrase such as 'all my estates at Clifton', but for every new acquisition, the will had to be rewritten. With this exception, disposal of unsettled real estate by will was in England unrestricted[100] and often arranged secretly. When the duke of Newcastle wished to make his will in 1707, in one of the few published accounts of such an occasion (because it became part of a famous lawsuit) he made use of his lawyer-agent, Peter Walter. Late in August he called Walter to his study at Welbeck, told him in strict secrecy that he wished to make his will, and talked at length with him about its provisions. Walter was ordered to draw up the will, which he did overnight. The duke left most of his property to his brother's son, who became Thomas Holles, duke of Newcastle. Four years later the duke died, and his will, which had not been known to his wife and daughter, was challenged in the courts[101]. A later source gives an account of will-making in the Dodington family (relatives of the celebrated Bubb). When one eighteenth-century Dodington was making his will, he asked his lawyer if he could remember any Dodingtons who he had not included in the entail? A little boy playing in the corner of the room said 'put me in' and Dodington did so; as it turned out, the little boy eventually succeeded to the estates[102].

(iv) *Settlements on other occasions.* A quite arbitrary, or accidental, motive might move a man to settle his land. Such motives could include a severe illness, the unexpected birth of an heir, the inheritance of more land. A projected settlement involving the adoption of an heir is described in Sir Walter Calverley's memorandum book. Sir Hugh Calveley [*sic*] of Lea, Cheshire, wrote to Henry Calverley in 1648 of his desire to settle his lands upon Henry's grandson, Sir Hugh being 'very weake in body' and wishing to perpetuate his name or at least something very like his name. The settlement was never completed because of the Civil War[103]. Sir John Lowther, whose settlement and will are referred to below, made his 1701 settlement in favour of his younger son because Sir John was ill and also because he had decided to disinherit his elder son (see below, p.74). The Catholic Nicholas Blundell settled his estates as the 1715 Jacobite rebellion broke out, foreseeing difficult times for those of his religion[104]. Marmaduke Tunstall of Wycliffe Hall in North Yorkshire settled his fee simple estate in 1734. He did not want to marry, and he agreed to settle so that his younger brother could marry and settle a jointure on his wife: his younger brother being the probable sucessor[105].

7 The conservation of the settlement

Whatever the occasion of the making of the settlement, once it was executed, it was unbreakable until the tenant in tail came of age, except by private act of Parliament (or, in a very small number of instances, where it contained provisions against the public interest, by a decision of Chancery). The execution of the deed was the final result of several drafts, read over to the parties. The reading over is mentioned several times by Sir Walter Calverley in his memorandum book; in one instance the bride wished to hear her marriage settlements read[106], and Calverley, as trustee to several settlements, used to note if he himself heard the deeds read. In 1654 when Sir Orlando Bridgeman had drawn a deed concerning Dorothy Osborne's portion, she went to his chambers and he began to read it to her: she said it was too long, and wanted only part of it read; she never read the whole deed before it was executed[107]. In the Sykes marriage settlement of 1822 the solicitors moved from one interested party to another, and duly charged for 'reading the settlements'[108]. This reading over seems to have been to check that the settlements did in fact contain what the family required, although anyone who has tried to listen to the reading of a long family settlement will understand how difficult that must have been.

Once executed, the deeds themselves were usually copied several times, to enable them to be readily consulted. The settlor kept one or more copies; the trustees had their own copy; the lawyers kept one or more copies. Great landowners often had muniment rooms in their houses, where such important documents as the settlements were kept[109]. In the Ridings of Yorkshire, in Middlesex and in the restricted area of the Hatfield level, summaries of settlements of real estate were registered in the deeds registries from the early eighteenth century. All wills (which often included settlements of real estate) were processed by the ecclesiastical courts and the originals stored or registered with the appropriate diocesan registry and from 1858 at Somerset House. Settlements were also of increasing interest to central government death duty officials as more legacies became taxable during the nineteenth century.

The settlement provided a framework, a constitution, for the family and the estates until such time as it was terminated. How many members of the family were aware of the terms of the settlement must have varied according to the character of the settlor: he may have concealed from his children what their income would be after his death, how much they would have as their portions, and what restrictions would be placed on their future life tenancies, in the same way that many wills were the secret, and often the secret weapon, of the testator. The heir, if he had joined in a resettlement, should have been aware of the terms, but members of the family outside the settlor and his heir might not know what was arranged;

Horace Walpole only found out by chance that the entail of the Orford estates had been altered[110]. In a case of 1800, a settlement of estates in Somerset had been concealed from the children by the parents, and after the parents' death, the deed itself was concealed by three daughters from the fourth[111]. A young man in the early seventeenth century recorded in his autobiography how he searched for the family settlements:

> My uncle Lancelot in his absence left me the keys of his chamber, where finding divers writings of my Grandfather's, as a deed of feoffment to the use of himself for life with remainder to my father in tail with power of revocation and divers leases and annuities made to his young sons and the same deed revoked, amongst others I found something by which it was likely that he had suspended his power of revocation and disabled himself to revoke of which taking advantage I copied the deeds and refused to give them to my uncle to whom they belonged not but gave them to my Grandfather Sir Richard . . .[112]

Although this example of detective work among the Lowther family is earlier than the period of strict settlement, it is a first-hand account of searches that must have been often carried out. A case about the estate of the Master of the Rolls in 1719 turned on the validity of articles of agreement for a marriage settlement which had never been executed: fifty years later the heir found the papers at the bottom of an old trunk, and persuaded Chancery to execute them[113].

The family lawyers and the estate administrators must have known some at least of the terms of settlement, for the settlement would necessarily be consulted before taking out a mortgage (since only specified purposes would be authorised, and the mortgagees would need to be assured of their title), or before drawing up a lease, for a lease not based upon a power would be void. In the nineteenth century the marquis of Stafford's solicitors granted long building leases on the unjustified assumption that the settlement allowed them[114]: but such mistakes cannot have been common. The agent of Sir James Graham of Netherby wrote in 1847 that his reluctance to borrow money for agricultural drainage was based on his knowledge of the family settlements and fear of increasing the incumbrances[115], and such knowledge must usually have been available to the estate agents.

(i) *The trustees.* The nominal guardians of the terms of the settlement were the trustees. The position of the trustees changed during the centuries of strict settlement, as the court tried to make them more responsible, although the judges were also conscious that too heavy a burden would make men more and more unwilling to accept the trust. Very frequently, according to Lord Hardwicke in 1750, the men who were named as trustees were not asked if they agreed to their nomination before being included in settlements[116], and often they refused to act when they discovered they had been named. In the seventeenth century Chancery tried to force men to accept trusteeships but this did not succeed[117]. Clearly an office, to which appointment could be made without prior agreement, was of little real significance. The courts did not allow a trustee payment for his time and trouble, because trustees should not benefit from their trust[118] although they were allowed expenses, and lawyer–trustees were allowed to charge for their professional work (but not for general trust business). Not consulted about their appointments, and not paid, the trustees expected to do very little work, and no class of professional trustee developed. In the majority of cases trustees were friends or relatives of the settlor, and any large collection of family papers will show the head of the family acting as trustee for the settlements of several neighbouring or related families. The mid-seventeenth century settlement of the Vavasours of Hazlewood, Yorkshire, printed in Bridgeman's *Conveyances*[119], named as trustees a son and a grandson of Lord Fauconberg, who were related to Vavasour's wife, and another unidentified knight. The Holkham estate trustees and guardians of 1707 were four relations; the Burton Constable trustees of 1791 were a neighbouring peer, a fellow Catholic squire and a London solicitor who acted for many Catholic families[120]. The practice of choosing local gentry or relations of the appropriate age is outlined by the solicitor/agent to the Burton Constable estates in 1827, when he suggested that the trustees should be 'young enough and settled enough to be probably living in the Country when Sir Clifford's children want their portions'[121]. The marquis of Ailesbury's trustees in 1832 were two cousins and the family solicitor[122]. The Sykes trustees of the various trusts of the 1847 settlement which included other trusts in addition to the preservation of contingent remainders were all related to the settlor or his wife. Three of the older generation were to act in the settlor's own trusts; two of the next generation were trustees for the settlor's children. The account books and papers show that the work of administering the active trusts of this settlement for the Sykes family was carried out by London solicitors[123].

The trustees did, however, normally have the ultimate legal responsibility for the trust. If they prejudiced the position of the person for whom the trust was intended (the legal phrase for this person was the *cestui que trust*) then the trustees were obliged to make the loss good, and in addition a breach of trust could be a criminal act. If a trustee sold trust lands, and the buyer knew there was a trust (he bought 'with notice') the buyer himself was bound by the same trust. If the trustee sold concealing the fact that there was a trust ('without notice'), the trustee himself could be made to buy other lands of the same value to be settled on the same trusts[124]; or, if the beneficiary of the trust preferred, he could take either the proceeds of the sale with interest, or the current estimated value of the land sold, after deducting any increases for subsequent improvements. Unauthorised exchanges, mortgages or leases were void.

If trustees and life tenant together breached the settlement, they could be made to compensate the trust estate: he who gained by the breach of the trust was ultimately liable to repay his gain[125].

(ii) *The lawyers*. At the beginning of the era of strict settlement the vital role of legal adviser in settlement matters was played by the barrister, who counselled the greater landed families, and both Orlando Bridgeman and Gilbert Horsman made fortunes in this way. London lawyers continued to be consulted in the making and interpretation of settlements right through the period: but attorneys and solicitors (the latter term becoming the more respectable) gradually took over the barristers' role. The status of attorney rose in the eighteenth and nineteenth centuries to meet the demands of the landowners, who expected their advisers to be a class of men 'to whom the property, honour, the confidence, and the affairs of men of family might be entrusted'[126]. The attorney Matthew Jermyn of George Eliot's *Felix Holt* (a novel set in 1832) who was acceptable – just – to the great family whose affairs he looked after, with his 'scented handkerchief and his charity-school Latin' had evolved by 1852 into the formidable family solicitor Mr Tulkinghorne of Dickens' *Bleak House,* who knew the secrets of many aristocratic families, and was a guest in the country houses of the great, where he not only dined but had his own bedroom. A leading conveyancing expert such as Jonathan Christie in 1844 was of sufficient status to retort to the duke of Buckingham (who had criticised Christie's proposals) 'I am wholly unaccustomed to the kind of censure implied in the tone which pervades his Grace's letter, & I shall take care not to expose myself to a repetition of similar comments'[127].

A common pattern on the larger landed estates seemed to be for families to employ a local solicitor for general business, a London solicitor for the most important work which would include the making of settlements, and in addition a conveyancing counsel for consultation. The Burton Constable estates in the late eighteenth and nineteenth centuries were organised for several generations by the Iveson family, solicitors in the nearest town of Hedon. The correspondence between the Ivesons and the Constables concerned the drafting and application of successive settlements, as well as estate business generally, and the Ivesons' role is much more significant than that of the trustees, who were mainly East Yorkshire landowners of equal or higher status than the Constables. London solicitors were also involved in the Constable settlements as trustees and as advisers, and the Ivesons sent their draft settlements to conveyancing counsel for approval[128]. An Iveson son served his articles in the London solicitors' office. Legal work from the Yorkshire family of Dawnay went to the same firm; if it were possible to find the complete records of a conveyancing practice, they might show that neighbouring or related families used the same London solicitors[129].

In another Yorkshire family, the Sykes of Sledmere, early nineteenth-century settlements were made, kept and interpreted by the local solicitors first in York and then in Beverley; but by the mid nineteenth century, although the local solicitors still kept the legal business of the family for every day estate matters, the making and administration of the settlements was conducted by London solicitors[130]. The tendency (which seems to have been consolidated by the late nineteenth century) to make settlement business separate from estate business was encouraged by the supersession of the farmer–bailiff and the estate solicitor by the emerging profession of the land agent, a class of men who were more concerned with farming than with the law.

8 Settlement problems and solutions

The implementation of a settlement which did not give rise to problems left little trace in the archives. But sometimes the settlement led to disputes; allegations that it had been obtained by undue influence, or that its provisions were unreasonable or against the public interest, and the family sought to overturn it. Alternatively, the settlement could be properly made, but the named heirs to the estate (the remaindermen) could find that the terms were being ignored, and that the life tenant, with or without the trustees, was selling land, granting unauthorised leases, or cutting down trees. In all these cases remedy could be sought through Chancery. The law itself would not prosecute a life tenant or a trustee for breaking the terms of the settlement: the action had to be set in motion by someone with an interest in the settlement. Records of such problems are to be found among the reports of cases in Chancery[131].

(i) *Undue influence.* Voluntary settlements obtained by undue influence could be held to be fraudulent, and set aside by the court. In certain relationships of trust (called 'fiduciary relationships') such as parent to child, guardian to ward, minister of religion to adherent, physician to patient, solicitor to client, in fact 'all the variety of relations in which dominion could be exercised by one person over another'[132] a settlement made by the dependent person in favour of the other was presumed to be the result of undue influence unless the beneficiary could prove otherwise. So that when in 1804 a middle-aged widow settled her estate at Hampton Gay in Oxfordshire on a clergyman, the Lord Chancellor decided subsequently that the clergyman had used his position as both her spiritual adviser and her agent to over-persuade her, and the court overturned the settlement[133]. In the case of Bunny Hall, however (see below, p.98) the courts did not overturn the settlement made on a man's mistress. In more normal situations where there was no fiduciary relationship, undue influence has, as always, to be proved by the complainant. In settlements made by will, the fiduciary relationship issue did not arise, and again the complainant had to prove the case.

(ii) *Unreasonable provisions.* Settlements could be made conditional: one of the commonest conditions was that if the future life tenants did not take the name and arms of the settlor, the estates would go to someone else[134]. An unreasonable condition could be negated by Chancery. Conditions restraining marriage were common: general prohibitions of marriage were void (as contrary to public policy), but conditions to marry or not marry a named person, a foreigner, a member of a different religion, or a member of a particular class such as a domestic servant, were valid, as were restrictions on marrying before a certain age, or marrying without parental permission[135]. A condition of the 1870 settlement of the Burton Constable estates was that the heir would give the family diamonds to his step-mother, and in addition settle some other estates in a prescribed manner[136]. For the courts to set aside such conditions they had either to be illegal or contrary to public policy, and these Burton Constable conditions were not contested. An unusual provision that *was* declared void (but only on appeal to the House of Lords) was that the inheritance of the Bridgewater estates could pass to the named heir and his descendants only if he obtained the title of duke or marquis of Bridgewater[137].

(iii) *Attainder.* The State itself was reluctant to set aside properly constituted settlements. One of the motives that was alleged to have encouraged the development of strict settlement was the fear of seventeenth-century landowners that they would lose the family's lands through backing the losing side in the Civil War. When a person convicted of treason or felony was sentenced to death or outlawed, he was 'attainted' and he lost his honours and his property[138]. However, if under a settlement he was only a life tenant, the estates continued in the possession of his heir. In the centuries after the Civil War, attainders were uncommon, but the device of settlement still operated effectively to cover such eventualities. In the Jacobite rebellions, several of the aristocracy were attainted[139]; the earl of Derwentwater lost his head and his earldom in 1716, but his son inherited the family estates[140]. The government was also careful to pay the settled amount of jointure to the widows of those it had executed and to make provision for their children[141]. In the same way that strict settlement could preserve the estates of attainted men, it was used, with the ingenuity of modern tax evasion, to protect Roman Catholic estates from the penalties of recusancy[142].

(iv) *Chancery*. The ultimate force which made life tenants and trustees conform to the provisions of the strict settlement was the equitable jurisdiction of the Lord Chancellor. But Chancery had no investigating office, no presenting juries, no policemen: breaches of the settlement had to be proved to the court by the next heirs, the remaindermen. And there were difficulties about that. It must have often been the case that the next heir, perhaps a cousin living in Scotland, or a nephew who was a small boy, had little idea what the settlement contained, and if the terms were being kept: perhaps the heir never visited the estate until after he inherited.

Sometimes the next heir may have consented to a breach of the settlement: for instance, the Sledmere life tenant in the 1820s increased his wife's jointure beyond the limit, having got his two brothers' agreement[143]. If a father and son together agreed to cut down a wood, even though grandfather had forbidden it, who would take them to court? The remote trustees might never know, or care, and the next heir was party to the breach. Chancery cases were never popular, for they were slow and expensive, and a family which indulged in a Chancery suit over settled land might find at the end of the case that there was nothing of value left to the successful suitor, and only the lawyers had won. Dickens, in *Bleak House,* paints a picture of Chancery at its very worst, in the first half of the nineteenth century, as *Jarndyce* v. *Jarndyce* winds on its interminable way, leaving in the end nothing for the litigants[144]. The threat to go to Chancery was enough to make the marquis of Chandos settle with his very difficult father[145]. Part of an appeal to a trustee to abandon separate representation in a Chancery suit in 1843 reads:

> You doubtless know that the property in question is VERY SMALL and that upwards of £500 has already been expended out of the Infant Earl's Estate in coming to the decision whether or not this proceeding should be taken . . . .[146]

Of the eleven landed families in East Yorkshire that had more than 10,000 acres in 1875, only four are known to have been involved in a Chancery suit connected with their settlements between 1660 and 1880[147]. It was apparently much commoner to obtain a private act of Parliament to alter the settlement, than to go to law over it[148]. It is not possible to make a precise analysis of all Chancery cases concerning strict settlement from the law reports because not all cases were reported, but only those of legal interest[149]. In a sample year, 1800, out of 104 reported cases in Chancery between 1 January and 31 December, only nine dealt with strict settlement in any material way[150]. Of these nine cases, all except one had been brought to the court by younger children or grandchildren of the settlor, who considered they had been injured by the way in which the settlement had been applied (the exception was a creditor, who brought a case with the agreement of the trustees to recover his money, the trustees' power to sell for such a purpose being imperfectly drafted). The commonest ground of complaint was that the power to apportion among the children had been improperly used[151]. Other grounds of complaint (not only in 1800, but generally) were the granting of unauthorised leases, portions or jointures, which were all types of fraud upon a power, and like all other cases alleging fraud, had to be proved by the person who sought to set aside the grant; and allegations that part of the inheritance had been wasted by the life tenant[152].

(v) *The private act of Parliament.* If a settlement became intolerable, the only way in which it could be altered before the tenant in tail came of age, was by a private act of Parliament. Private acts to regulate the tenure of property are recorded from 1512, and fall into six main categories, but the majority of private acts relate to the settlement of estates. From about 1660, as strict settlement became more common, estate acts to alter settlement increased in number, eventually so impeding the other work of Parliament that between 1698 and 1706 a code of Standing Orders was worked out by the Lords to deal with them[153]. 167 estate acts were passed in the reign of Charles II, an average of seven a year. In James II's reign only two received the royal assent: but there was only one year in which Parliament assembled. An average of 26 estate acts a year passed in William and Mary's reign, and an average of 29 in Anne's reign. These figures of about 20–30 acts per year continued through the eighteenth and first half of the nineteenth century. Between 1867 and 1884 the number declined to about seven a year because by this time a number of enabling acts had been passed by Parliament giving wider powers to all life tenants[154]. To quote one final figure to show the heavy load of private legislation (which included many other categories beside estate acts): between 1800 and 1884 there were 9556 public acts, but 18,497 private acts[155].

Estate bills were usually introduced into the House of Lords first and there referred to two judges. They passed through both Houses, were read three times in each, and sent to Select Committee in each before they received royal assent. It sounds a slow business, but in fact a bill, even if opposed, could pass in a matter of weeks[156]. Almost any difficulty arising in the management of a settled estate could be remedied by private act, and landowners both great and small applied for them. The private estate act was cheaper to obtain and a much faster process than a suit in Chancery. Instead of being at the mercy of the lawyers, an estate bill went before two bodies of men who were almost exclusively landowners themselves. The archives of most large landed families will show at least one private estate act to modify the settlements, and often more than one. Between 1801 and 1880 alone, the eleven major East Riding landed families together obtained eleven private estate acts.

For some types of alteration of settlements by private estate act, the year 1800 has again been chosen as an example. That year 25 English private estate bills were brought into Parliament, and, in most cases amended by the legislature, they all received royal assent in the same year. All but one dealt with settled landed estates (the exception was the duke of Richmond's bill to charge a government annuity that he held with a jointure!) and the purpose of about half the bills (fourteen) was to enable the trustees and tenants for life to sell settled estates for various purposes such as paying off incumbrances or raising purchase money for other lands, to be settled to the same uses. Partition and exchange were powers sought less commonly, in five cases. The appointment of new trustees was the object of two bills. Lord Guilford asked for a power to raise portions for his children, and the trustees of the Pulteney estate wished to charge the repair of the bridge at Bath to the estate. One bill was to enable the trustees and tenant for life to enfranchise copyhold and grant leases, and two to enable them to sell or lease building and mining land[157].

After the middle of the nineteenth century the annual number of private estate acts diminished, for a series of enabling acts passed through Parliament, designed to help life tenants out of some of the restrictions of settlement: the enabling acts gave all life tenants the kind of powers most commonly sought in private acts. The first of these, Pusey's Drainage Act of 1840, empowered tenants for life and other limited owners to charge the expenses of land drainage to the inheritance. The 1840 act was not much used, but was followed by other more effective drainage acts in the succeeding decades. Through the 1850s, 1860s and 1870s other acts allowed life tenants to raise money on their estates for a wide range of improvements[158]. Parliament had since the eighteenth century accepted clauses in the appropriate acts allowing limited owners to charge their estates with the expenses of public works activities such as enclosure, canal building, and eventually railway works. Without such powers life tenants would have been severely hampered in this type of development by their lack of capital[159].

Until 1857 divorce and legal separation required a private act of Parliament, a process which virtually restricted their use to the propertied class and was in any case never common. When a marriage ended, marriage settlements had to be ended in the same way and the property jointly settled had to be divided up again, with fresh provision for the ex-wives in lieu of jointure. In 1700 the duke of

Norfolk succeeded in divorcing his wife (she claimed that he had brought the bill because she refused to join in the sale of certain estates, to relieve him of money difficulties). The marriage settlement settling the jointure and lands for the duchess's use was set aside by both parties, and she was to receive £10,000 in lieu[160]. Sir George Downing, 3rd baronet, was refused a divorce by the House of Lords, but succeeded in obtaining a private act to ratify his settlement with his wife on their separation[161].

Chapter II Reality

1 Some settlement patterns

In practice the history of any one family's settlements showed a rich variety of types and occasions of settlements, and a number of occasions when part or the whole estate was not under settlement. In many families the pattern of settlement of one group of lands might be different from that of another group: for instance, the duke of Devonshire's estates in 1717 lay in the counties of Derbyshire, Huntingdonshire, Lancashire, Nottinghamshire, Staffordshire and Yorkshire and were governed by separate settlements of 1674, 1678 and 1694[162]. The estates of earl Fitzwilliam in 1782 were in three parts, for that was how they had been inherited: part of the Irish estate, the Wentworth Woodhouse estate and the Milton estate were all settled separately[163]. On the lands of Lord Downe in the nineteenth century the settlements of the North and West Riding estates differed from those of the Wykeham estate, also owned by the Downes, in the North and East Ridings[164]. The duke of Buckingham in 1847 held settled estates under two different settlements, and also unsettled land[165]. Under settlements made at different times, a man might be simultaneously life tenant on one estate, and tenant in tail on another: a situation illustrated in the Bower family (see below, pp.71–3).

Almost all estates had some land unsettled at any time: land that had been left deliberately out of the last settlement, or land that had been bought since the last settlement was made. A whole estate could become unsettled through disentailing by a tenant in tail who chose not to resettle, for settlement was not inevitably renewed to create a form of perpetual entail. It was also possible to leave land either unsettled or settled subject to a general power of appointment for long periods (see above, pp.29–30).

(i) *Coke of Holkham*

The Coke family were for many decades the leading landowning family of Norfolk, and famous agriculturalists. The founder of the family fortunes was Sir Edward Coke, the lawyer (1552–1634), who bought lands in many counties and settled them on his various children. After his death, the Cokes continued to acquire land, with the family pursuing a long-term policy of buying in North Norfolk to build up the estate, and by 1883 they owned 44,000 acres, centred around a great house at Holkham[166].

John Coke (grandson of Sir Edward) inherited Holkham and the main Norfolk estate as tenant in tail in 1661 on the death of his father, another John, who had been tenant for life since 1653[167]. As tenant in tail in possession, he could easily disentail his estates and obtain a fee simple: presumably he did so (although the deed has not been traced) for in 1665 he possessed a fee simple, which he then proceeded to settle strictly 'in his owne and the name family and Bloud of Sir Edward Coke late Lord Cheiffe Justice . . . his grandfather'[168]. He entailed all his lands on Coke relatives in succession and in tail male (living Cokes taking life tenancies, and unborn heirs being tenants in tail, with contingent remainders protected by trustees). After John Coke's own death, without issue male (he was unmarried) the order of succession read:

Richard Coke of Thorington
Robert son of Richard Coke of Thorington
1st and other sons of Robert
Other sons of Richard Coke and issue male
Roger Coke of London
1st and other sons of Roger
Cyriack Coke of Beccles
Henry 1st son of Cyriack Coke
1st and other sons of Henry
John 2nd son of Cyriack Coke
1st and other sons of John
Cyriack 3rd son of Cyriack Coke
1st and other sons of Cyriack Coke the son
Other sons of Cyriack Coke the father and issue male
Sir Edward Coke of Longford

Robert 1st son of Sir Edward Coke
1st and other sons of Robert
Edward 2nd son of Sir Robert Coke
1st and other sons of Edward
Other sons of Sir Edward and issue male
Robert Coke of Nonsuch
Clement 1st son of Robert Coke
1st and other sons of Clement
Robert 2nd son of Robert Coke
1st and other son of Robert Coke the son
Other sons of Robert Coke the father and issue male
Right heirs of John Coke and settlor[169]

In 1665 Coke reserved the power of granting leases at Holkham and on other lands and manors in Norfolk and Suffolk. In 1671 he used his power to lease these, in trust to pay his debts, funeral expenses and legacies[170].

John Coke died in 1671. He was succeeded as life tenant by the 2nd man named in the entail, his cousin Robert, son of the now deceased Richard Coke of Thorington. The lands that Sir Edward Coke had in 1634 divided between his children were now for the most part united in the hands of Robert Coke. Robert married in 1674, and, as under John Coke's settlement he had the power to do, he charged lands in Suffolk, Dorset, Somerset and Stafford with his wife's jointure[171]. There was some ambiguity about John Coke's settlement of 1665, and in 1678 Robert Coke obtained a private act of Parliament to allow him to make leases and to provide for daughters' portions and payment of his debts. The act received the royal assent on 20 March 1678 (new style) and was entitled 'An Act to supply the Defects in a Deed of Settlement made by John Coke Esquire deceased and for altering a Trust in Part of the Estate of Robert Coke'[172].

Robert's son Edward Coke, who was the tenant in tail of John Coke's settlement of 1665, was born in 1676 and succeeded, aged three, on the death of his father in 1679[173]. Edward married in 1696 when he was only 20, and being still under age had to obtain a special warrant to disentail all his lands in order to make a settlement on his marriage[174]. All the Coke estates, manors and lands in Norfolk and elsewhere were settled at this marriage of 1696[175], and the lands continued to be governed by the marriage settlement (although Edward himself died in 1707) until Edward's son Thomas came of age in 1718, when he immediately disentailed, the day after his twenty-first birthday[176]. About two weeks later Thomas (who was later to be created earl of Leicester) married and some of the lands were resettled. In the same year the dowager of the family, Thomas Coke's grandmother, assigned her jointure estate which she had held since her husband's death in 1679 to her grandson, in return for an annuity of £1200 a year for her life[177].

On Thomas Coke's marriage in July 1718 most of the Norfolk estates were settled, but lands in the other counties were left unsettled. Properties in some 83 places in Norfolk were assigned to trustees. As was the custom on some large estates, lands were settled for different purposes: property in 12 places out of the 83 was charged with the bride's pin-money, property in 32 other places was assigned to secure the jointure, and property in a further 32 places (including those 12 also charged with pin-money, but not including any of the jointure lands) was assigned to raise portions for younger children. These arrangements left some 19 Norfolk places with no specific charge on them in settlement, and the substantial estates outside Norfolk unsettled[178]. After these uses, the land settled in Norfolk was entailed on the first and every other son of the marriage in tail male, with various remainders over.

The settlement of 1718 ended in 1747 and a new one was made, on the marriage of Thomas Coke's son Edward. Edward, who was tenant in tail of the 1718 settlement, had come of age in 1740 and could have with his father's consent disentailed from that year; but it was not until his marriage was arranged that the disentailing and resettlement took place. It was a complex resettlement, as the family wished to alter the pin-money, dower and portion arrangements of 1718, which would not have been annulled by the docking of the entail, but could only be done by private act of Parliament[179]. Again, only the Norfolk lands were settled, and not all of these. The sums granted in 1718 for pin-money, jointure and portions continued, but were now all charged on the same lands (instead of being divided between land for pin-money, land for jointure and land for portions), and the list of places named in 1747 was in some cases different from those named in 1718. The heir Edward and his bride were also provided for, and enabled to raise jointure and portions of their own. The entail established by the settlement of 1718 was ended; the new entail now established gave a life interest to Thomas Coke, a future life interest to Edward Coke, and named Edward's eldest son and other sons in succession born to the 1747 marriage as tenant in tail, with remainder to Edward's eldest son and other sons in succession born of any later marriage, with final remainder to Thomas Coke (the life tenant at the time the settlement was made) in fee simple.

As it turned out, Edward Coke died in 1753, in his father's lifetime, without any children. That meant that the entail established in 1747 brought the final remainder of the estates back to Thomas Coke who now possessed the fee simple of all his lands, subject to the payments of pin-money and future jointure to his wife, and jointure to his daughter-in-law. There were no younger children, so no portions were necessary.

Thomas Coke lived on until 1759, having been created earl of Leicester in 1744. He had no surviving children, and by his will, made in 1756, he settled all his estate strictly, on a succession of life tenants. First his widow had a life interest; after her the next life tenant was the earl's nephew, Wenham Coke, who succeeded the dowager countess in 1775; a year later, when Wenham died, his son Thomas William Coke (known as Coke of Norfolk) succeeded to the estates, also as a life tenant, for he had been born in his great uncle's lifetime and was therefore named in the earl's will as tenant for life and not tenant in tail[180]. Thomas Coke's eldest son was tenant in tail of the 1759 settlement, but as he was born late in his father's life (to his second marriage) Thomas William Coke did not live to see a tenant in tail of full age who could join him in disentailing.

Coke of Norfolk, who had succeeded in 1776, lived until 1842; and during all these years he was a life tenant under the will proved in 1759. The will was very restrictive, as nothing except jointures could be charged to the settled estates[181]. Coke did, however, obtain three private acts of Parliament to allow him to modify the settlement for specific reasons: which were, to sell some land and to buy other land which was settled to the same uses, and to allow him to exchange some of his own unsettled land with the trustees of his settled estates[182]. Towards the end of his long life Coke of Norfolk was created an earl, and became the 1st earl of Leicester of Holkham (as contrasted with his great uncle, whose title of earl of Leicester had died with him). When Coke of Norfolk died, his son and heir was still under age, and as his son wished to marry, another private act was obtained in 1843 to enable him to charge the estates with a jointure[183].

In December 1843 the 2nd earl of Leicester of Holkham came of age, and as tenant in tail in possession under the 1759 settlement, he (in April 1844) disentailed all the settled estates[184]. The estates were left unsettled in the hands of the 2nd earl from the disentailing of 1844 until his death in 1909, when his will (made in 1897) came into effect and strictly settled the estates. During the years from 1844 to 1909 there were two marriage settlements. The first was in 1875 (the second marriage of the earl) and the second in 1879 (when the heir, later the 3rd earl, married) but neither of these marriage settlements, nor the earlier arrangements on marriage made by the private act of 1843, entailed the estates, but merely provided jointures and portions[185].

The 1909 will devised particular manors on the 2nd earl's widow for her life and some properties in strict settlement on younger sons, in tail male. All the remaining lands (the great majority) were strictly settled, first on the 3rd earl for his life, then on the 3rd earl's eldest son for his life, in tail male, with remainders over. No son of the 3rd earl living at the time the will was proved was to have more than a life estate[186]. Although the later history of the settlement is outside the scope of this present enquiry, it appears that the 1909 will settled the estates until about 1968.

Descent of the Coke family of Holkham

John Coke
d.1671

Robert
1651–1679

Edward
1676–1707

Thomas
earl of Leicester
1697–1759
= Margaret
1700–1775

Edward
1719–1753

Anne
d.1758
= Philip Roberts

Wenham (Roberts) Coke
1717–1776

Thomas William
1st earl of Leicester of Holkham
1754–1842

Thomas William
2nd earl of Leicester of Holkham
1822–1909

Thomas William
3rd earl of Leicester of Holkham
1848–1941

Thomas William
4th earl of Leicester of Holkham
1880–1949

Thomas William Edward
5th earl of Leicester of Holkham
1908–1976

Settlement history of the Cokes (earls of Leicester, of Holkham) (Norfolk estates)

Before 1661	settled
1661–1665	unsettled
1665–1696	strictly settled by deed of 1665, amended by private act of 1678
1696–1718	strictly settled by marriage settlement of 1696
1718–1747	part strictly settled by marriage settlement of 1718, part unsettled
1747–1753	part strictly settled by marriage settlement and private act of 1747, part unsettled
1753–1759	fee simple
1759–1844	strictly settled by will proved 1759, modified by 4 private acts
1844–1909	fee simple after disentailing of 1844
1909–1968	strictly settled by will proved 1909

(ii) *The Grosvenors in Westminster*

Three hundred years ago the Grosvenor family, Cheshire baronets, acquired through marriage a small estate of about 500 acres to the west of London, as a result of which they became ultimately the richest urban landlords in Britain. The London estate came into the Grosvenor family (later dukes of Westminster) through the marriage in 1677 of Sir Thomas Grosvenor, 3rd baronet, with Mary Davies, the twelve-year-old daughter and heiress of Alexander Davies, a London scrivener. Davies's daughter was less than six months old when her father died of the plague in 1665, and two years earlier he had settled the estate on trustees for the benefit first of himself and then of his heirs. As Mary Davies was under age at the time of her marriage, no resettlements of her lands could be made, and her father's arrangements continued to govern the estate until 1694, seventeen years after her marriage and after the birth of her two sons. A new and strict settlement was made in 1694; and it is surprising that the settlement was so long delayed, for it could have been made at any time after the bride was of age, or earlier by private act of Parliament. Neither the bride's majority nor the birth of an heir produced a settlement. Mary Davies's insanity was only apparent after the settlement of 1694, and was not the reason for the postponement. It appears, however, from the correspondence of the heiress that she enjoyed the partial control she had over the estate under her father's arrangements, and was in no hurry to give this up[187]. From the Grosvenors' point of view, the London estate in the later seventeenth century was not of great significance in their total landholdings.

After the death of Sir Thomas Grosvenor in 1700, there were difficulties with the dower lands of the two widows (Mary Davies and her mother). A private act in 1711 allowed an alteration in the 1694 arrangements. On the death of the dowagers, the 4th baronet disentailed the estate by the legal process of a common recovery and held it as a fee simple from 1730 to 1732: but he then strictly settled it once more by his will which came into effect on his death in 1732.

The 1732 settlement lasted through the lives of the 5th and 6th baronets (brothers of the 4th baronet), and was ended by the tenant in tail, the 7th baronet, in 1755, the year in which he succeeded. The 7th baronet (later the 1st earl Grosvenor) kept the estate unsettled, as a fee simple, until his debts forced him to make it over to trustees. This was an arrangement which was not uncommon in times of financial emergency, and while it was not equivalent to a settlement, such a trust restricted the landowner's powers. His son, the 1st marquis, cleared the remaining debts and dissolved the trust in 1808, and held a fee simple of all his estates until, at his death in 1845, they were once more strictly settled by his will: a settlement which entailed the London estate on the marquis's son and grandson as successive life tenants, and then on his (as yet unborn) great-grandson as tenant-in-tail. When the great-grandson came of age in 1874 the estate was disentailed and immediately resettled, and the settlement lasted until 1901[188].

The settlements outlined above were those of the London property, which became the principal source of the great wealth of the Grosvenors. The family owned estates elsewhere in England and Wales, which were not always settled in the same way: in 1711, for instance, the Grosvenor estates in Middlesex, Cheshire, Denbigh and Flint were settled partly on the widow of Alexander Davies as dower, partly on the daughter of Alexander Davies as dower (she was the widow of Thomas Grosvenor, 3rd baronet) and partly on the 4th baronet and his wife in tail male[189]. In 1869 the 3rd marquis (later the 1st duke) of Westminster was life tenant, under a strict settlement, of the whole of the London estate and part of the Cheshire, Chester and Halkyn estates. He also inherited the fee simple of Eaton Hall, Halkyn Castle and the bulk of the Cheshire, Chester and Flint properties, but the Dorset and Wiltshire properties which had been held by his father as unsettled lands were left to his widow for her life and then the Dorset lands were to pass to her younger son and the Wiltshire lands to her son-in-law[190].

The summary of the London properties alone produces the following pattern of settlement:

Settlement history of the London estate of the Grosvenors (dukes of Westminster)

1663–1694	settled by deed of 1663
1694–1711	strictly settled by deed of 1694
1711–1730	strictly settled by private act 1711
1730–1732	fee simple after disentailing of 1730
1732–1755	strictly settled by will proved 1732
1755–1779	fee simple after disentailing of 1755
1779–1808	in trust to pay debts, by deeds of 1779, 1785
1808–1845	fee simple after trust dissolved in 1808
1845–1874	strictly settled by will proved 1845
1874–1901	strictly settled by resettlement of 1874

(iii) *The Hothams, East Yorkshire baronets and barons*

The settlements of the East Yorkshire family of the Hothams illlustrate the complexity of settlement in general, and also some particular complications due to family circumstances. In spite of vicissitudes, the family built up its estates over the decades by purchase and inheritances, and by 1883 held some 20,000 acres in Yorkshire[191].

In 1680 the 2nd baronet had made a strict settlement on the marriage of his son and heir (John, who became the 3rd baronet) by which one manor was settled on the marriage with immediate effect to provide an income for John and a jointure for his wife if she survived him, and all other lands (except one property) were settled on the 2nd baronet for life, with an ultimate remainder or reversion to John's heirs[192]. The one property left out of the 1680 settlement, together with the estate of South Dalton which was bought in 1680 and eventually became the principal family residence, were devised by the will of the 2nd baronet (made 1682, proved 1689) to his widow. In 1687, in an unusual arrangement, the 2nd baronet conveyed his life interest in the estates to trustees, to pay an annuity to his wife: this seems to have been a precaution to avoid some of the consequences of a threatened confiscation because of his politics[193]. The estates were indeed confiscated by the Crown in 1688, but this confiscation was revoked in the same year by the new king, William III[194].

Before the death of the 2nd baronet his son had separated from his wife (in 1687) and the ultimate remainder that had been set out in the marriage settlement was altered. The young man now gave up some of the future rights in the property to his parents: that is, he kept his own (future) life interest and the rights of his (never born) sons, but renounced potential future rights (the ultimate remainder or reversion) beyond his own life and that of his sons: in the words of the deed he gave up the 'remainder or reversion in fee onely and not his present estate or remainder in taile'[195].

In 1689 the 2nd baronet died. His son was now 3rd baronet and tenant for life, under the 1680 marriage settlement, but his mother, the widowed Lady Elizabeth Hotham, held the right of reversion to the family estates in the event of her son dying childless, an event which now seemed probable. The 3rd baronet was separated from his wife, in poor health, heavily in debt and at loggerheads with his mother: she chose, in 1689, to settle the reversion on her husband's next male relative Charles Hotham 'for the support of the family and name of Hotham' in tail male, with remainder to her daughter's relations by marriage, members of the Gee family, if they would take the name of Hotham. By doing so she was exercising her rights under her son's renunciation of 1687, but perhaps she was not certain about her arrangements, for she kept a power of revocation of this settlement[196]: and she used this power in 1690 to revoke it and make a new settlement on Charles Hotham, because he had in the meantime married Bridget Gee 'and . . . other thinges have likewise

Descent of the Hothams

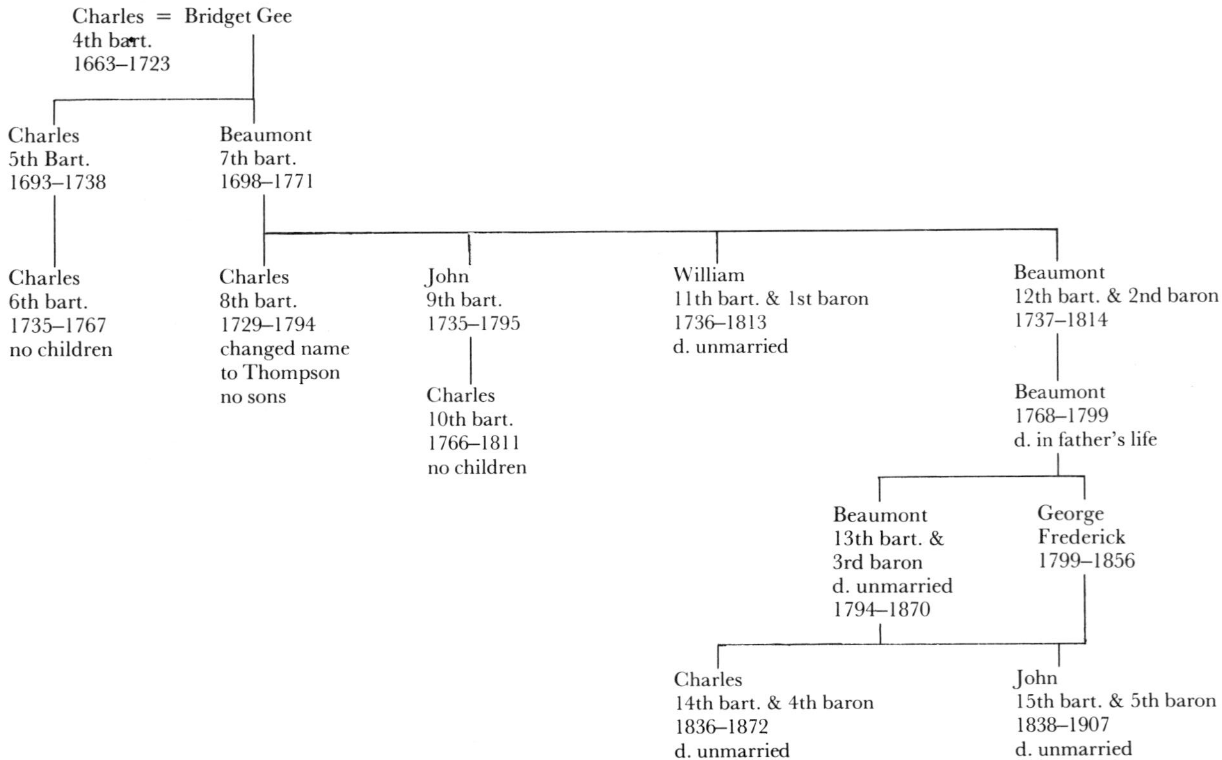

happened'[197]. It is clear from the dates of the deeds that Lady Hotham had originally given Charles the provisional reversion to the estates before the marriage was agreed.

The new settlement of 1690, instead of merely settling the reversion to the estates on Charles for life and then in tail male, laid down that after his death the reversion would pass to Bridget his widow, in augmentation of her jointure, and then in tail male. The reversion was still only a future interest, which might never have become a reality. But in 1691 John, the 3rd baronet, did die without children: Lady Elizabeth's interests in the estates had already been enlarged, for in the last year of his life her son had assigned all the rents of his estates to her in order to pay his debts[198]. At John's death Charles Hotham became the 4th baronet and tenant for life of the family estates, subject to Lady Elizabeth's life interest as dowager. The 1690 settlement was reinforced by the will of Lady Elizabeth (made and proved in 1697) by which she gave the dower lands previously devised to her by her husband and any residual rights from earlier arrangements to Charles Hotham in fee simple[199].

The 1690 settlement lasted until 1720, when Charles (whose wife Bridget had died in 1707) and his eldest son, also Charles and then aged 27, disentailed and resettled the estates, granting them to the father for life and then to his son in fee[200]. When Charles, 5th baronet, inherited in 1724 on the death of his father, he went through legal process of suffering a common recovery to give himself a clear title and then settled the estates strictly on his marriage in the same year. He married a daughter of the earl of Chesterfield, a marriage that was very important in the history of the family fortunes 'both financially and socially'[201], and the 1724 settlement was an example, less common than is sometimes supposed, of the whole of the estates being strictly settled at marriage[202].

The 1724 deed named the first son of the marriage as tenant in tail: this boy, the 6th baronet, was only three years old when his father died in 1738, so that throughout his minority the estates were governed by the trustees of the marriage settlement. He came of age in 1755 and (as he was tenant in tail in possession and could break the entail) disentailed and then held the estates as a fee simple from at least 1757[203] for the rest of his life. On his death in 1767, without children, his relatives and their solicitors were unable to find his will, and it was only discovered after some months' search[204]. Until it was found no one knew who would inherit the estates; but once discovered, the will showed that the estates were strictly settled to follow the descent of the baronetcy, to the uncle of the deceased baronet and the uncle's sons, who were to become 7th, 8th and 9th baronets. At this period several baronets died soon after inheriting, and the succession may be illustrated by a family tree (p.64).

The entail established by the will of 1767 was broken in 1787, by a combination of the 8th baronet (who had no sons), his brother the apparent next life tenant and his son Charles, who had just come of age and who was described in the disentailing and resettlement deeds of 1787 as 'entitled in remainder expectant': that is, he would be tenant in tail if his uncle died without male heirs[205]. This unusual (and probably illegal) combination of uncle, uncle's brother and eldest nephew disentailed the estate. It was very doubtful whether an expectant tenant in tail had the right to bar the entail[206]. The trustees to preserve the contingent remainders were included in a strict settlement to prevent this kind of disentailing, for the combination of uncle, uncle's brother and nephew excluded the uncle's son from inheriting under the 1767 settlement. In fact he never had any sons: but the sons he might have fathered during the rest of his life were part of the 'contingent remainders' who should have been protected.

The trustees' doubtful position was, however, rectified when the resettlement which followed immediately on the 1787 disentailing restored the *status quo* of the old settlement as far as the entail was concerned, except that (and this was the purpose of the entire transaction) the nephew and his cousin, who had formerly been tenants in tail, now became tenants for life. The resettlement granted a life tenancy to the 8th baronet, a tenancy in tail to his son if any were born, and if there should be no son (which was the case), successive life tenancies to the next brother of the 8th baronet (who became the 9th baronet), his son (the 10th baronet), a tenancy in tail to the sons of the 10th baronet (none was born), and successive life tenancies to the remaining brothers of the 8th baronet, who became the 11th and 12th baronets, with successive remainders to their sons and sons' sons, if any, as tenants for life if they were alive in 1787, as tenants in tail if they were born subsequently[207].

The 1787 settlement lasted through the life tenancies of the 8th, 9th, 10th, 11th and 12th baronets. The 12th baronet outlived his son (who in any case would have been another life tenant as he was born before 1787) so that the first tenant in tail with power to disentail was the grandson of the 12th baronet. During this period the family had acquired an Irish barony, so that the 12th baronet was also the 2nd baron. At the death of the 12th baronet in 1814 his grandson and successor was still a minor, but in 1817, two years after he came of age, he disentailed and immediately resettled, thus ending the 1787 settlement and imposing a new one. Between the death of the 6th baronet in 1767 and the disentailing carried out by the 13th baronet in 1817 there had been seven life tenants under strict settlement, and only one occasion in 1787 when the family held the fee simple (and that probably unlawfully).

The 1817 disentailing and immediate resettlement was in accordance with the will of the 11th baronet (and 1st baron) who had left his own property to his great nephew on condition that he resettled the family estates strictly within two years of coming of age[208]. This is a good example (which can be found in other families too) of inducements offered to tenants in tail to make new settlements. In 1817 therefore once again the estates were strictly settled, although by 1870 there were also unsettled lands which must have been bought or inherited since 1817, or perhaps simply left out of the 1817 settlement[209].

The 13th baronet (3rd baron) was tenant for life under the 1817 settlement until his death, unmarried, in 1870. Like the 11th baronet, he too wished 'that the settled estates should be resettled so as to be enjoyed for as long a period as the law would allow by the person entitled to the Barony of Hotham' and so by his will, which was proved in 1871, he devised his own settled land and his personal fortune to trustees upon trust, in case a resettlement of the settled estates took place, to settle the land and buy other land to be settled to the same uses and trusts as the settled estates should be subject to on resettlement. The 3rd baron was succeeded in the settled estates by his nephew. He was tenant in tail of the 1817 settlement, but in

May 1872 in accordance with his uncle's will, he disentailed and resettled, giving himself a life tenancy[210]. He died unmarried and was succeeded by his brother, who also died unmarried in 1907[211].

Settlement history of the Hothams (baronets and later barons)

1680–1691	settled by marriage settlement of 1680
1691–1720	settled by deeds of 1689, 1690 and will proved 1697
1720–1724	disentailed and resettled in 1720
1724–1757	disentailed 1724 and strictly resettled on marriage
1757–1767	fee simple
1767–1787	strictly settled by will proved 1767
1787–1817	disentailed and strictly settled on heir's majority
1817–1872	disentailed and strictly settled 1817 on heir's majority
1872–1907?	disentailed and strictly settled on heir inheriting

(iv) *The Downing estates*

Sir George Downing, the 1st baronet (1625–1684) was a soldier and diplomat, one of the first graduates of Harvard College, and reputed to be one of the richest men in seventeenth-century England. He gave his name to Downing Street, and his grandson founded Downing College, Cambridge. During his lifetime Sir George bought much land, mainly in Cambridgeshire, Suffolk and Bedfordshire, which he held in fee simple, and acquired land in Westminster held on long lease[212].

In August 1683 the 1st baronet settled most of his country property on the marriage of his eldest son and heir (George, later 2nd baronet, 1656–1711). He made provision for his son's maintenance and the bride's jointure, and having done so, in order to carry out his intention of 'settling and continuing of the manors . . . in the name, family and blood of Sir George Downing' he granted to trustees lands in the counties of Cambridge, Suffolk, Bedford, Huntingdon and Norfolk for the use of himself for life, then in strict settlement on his son George for life and to the 1st, 2nd and other sons of the marriage in tail male, with remainders to the other sons of the 1st baronet for their lives and thereafter in tail male[213]. By the 1st baronet's will, also made in 1683 and proved in 1684, he devised certain lands left out of the strict settlement. He used a power included in the marriage settlement to appoint lands worth £400 to his son George and other lands worth £400 to his son William. He disposed of his leasehold property in Downing Street and elsewhere in London to his younger sons Charles and William, and their children, severally and in succession with final remainder to George his heir. Land not included in the marriage settlement was to provide maintenance and portions for his three daughters, any surplus and the final remainder of this land to pass to his two younger sons and their children: his son Charles was to have all Sir George's lands in New England, with remainder to Charles's children, William and his children, George the heir and his children, and finally to the right heirs of the 1st baronet[214].

The tenant in tail of the 1683 settlement of the main estates was the eldest son of the 2nd baronet's marriage, George, later 3rd baronet (1685–1749). No disentailing seems to have taken place when he came of age in 1706, perhaps because father and son lived apart, the 2nd baronet being accounted 'not of sound mind' and also excommunicated for adultery[215]. The 2nd baronet made an elaborate will in 1688 arranging (among other things) that at his death his personal estate should be used to buy land to be strictly settled on his son when he became 25, in tail male, with remainders over[216]. This will, however, was never proved, and the 3rd baronet was granted letters of administration in 1713, eighteen months after his father's death, as if his father had died intestate. A late eighteenth-century abstract of title recited the will of 1688 as if it might have been relevant to the title, but then noted that administration was granted to the 3rd baronet 'although the above Will was in his possession'[217].

In his youth George Downing, later the 3rd baronet, had been married under age to his guardian's daughter: about the year 1701, when he was fifteen and his bride thirteen. The ceremony was secret, and there was apparently no marriage settlement[218]. The marriage was never consummated and ultimately both parties asked for a divorce, which was refused by the House of Lords in 1715. They continued to live separately, as they had always done; but in 1716 the couple agreed to disentangle their affairs (she giving up common law dower rights in return for the establishment of a trust fund for her separate use) and in 1718 the articles of agreement by which they did this were confirmed by a private act of Parliament[219]. Later abstracts of title of the Downing estates begin from a series of recoveries of 1716, the articles of agreement of 1716 and the private act: the position between 1711 and 1716 was never clarified, as the fee simple established in 1716, and its confirmation in the private act, provided an impeccable base for all future title deeds[220].

It was probably in connection with his matrimonial affairs that in December 1717 Sir George Downing, 3rd baronet, made a will devising his lands (about 9550 acres) in the counties of Cambridge, Bedford and Suffolk in strict settlement on four male cousins. The land was devised to five trustees, for the use of Jacob Downing for life, then to his 1st son and the heirs male of the body of such son: and in default of such issue to the use of the 2nd, 3rd, 4th, 5th and every son of Jacob Downing severally and successively in remainder one after another and the heirs male of such sons, in priority according to age: each stage being protected by the interposition of trustees to preserve the contingent remainders. At the time the will was made, Jacob was about one year old. If Jacob Downing died and had no male heir to inherit, the estates were to pass to Thomas Barnardiston and his sons in tail male; with remainder to Charles Peters and his sons in tail male: with remainder to John Peters and his sons in tail male: all severally and successively, the elder always taking before the younger. Every male person in possession of the estates had to take the surname of Downing only. If there was no issue male in these four lines, the final remainder was to the trustees and their heirs, in trust, to buy land in Cambridge and build there a college of the university to be called Downing's College[221]. When the will was made in 1717, there must have seemed little likelihood of the college being founded. Jacob Downing was a baby: the other cousins were all young men. However, as it turned out, none of these four men was to father a son.

The 3rd baronet died in 1749, 32 years after making his will. His cousin, Sir Jacob Downing, the 4th and last baronet, succeeded to the title and the life interest in the estates under the 1717 will, but when he died in 1764 he left no children. The other three cousins had died before Sir Jacob, without producing sons, so that by 1764 all the male lines named in the will were extinct. The estates should now have been used to found the college: but the 4th baronet by his will had left everything he possessed, including the property he had inherited from his cousin George, to his wife, as if the ultimate remainder to the trustees to found a new college did not exist. The original trustees of the 1717 will were all dead, and the widow of Sir Jacob Downing refused to give up the estates. It required a Chancery case, brought on behalf of the university of Cambridge, to enforce the terms of the 1717 will, and even though Chancery decided in favour of the university in 1769, the widow of the 4th baronet, and subsequently her nephew (to whom she had devised her possession of the estates) managed to keep the property until 1800. In 1800 Downing College received its charter, and in 1807 the foundation stone was finally laid[222].

Settlement history of the Downing estates

Before 1683	unsettled
1683–1711	strictly settled by marriage settlement of 1683 and will proved 1684
1711–1716	position uncertain: tenant in tail in possession
1716–1749	fee simple following recoveries and articles of agreement of 1716, confirmed by private act of 1718
1749–1764	strictly settled by will dated 1717, proved 1749
1764–1800	estates disputed in Chancery after death without issue of all possible devisees named in entail
1800	estates confirmed to the new college

(v) *The Bowers of Welham, East Yorkshire*

In many families inheritances came from different sources, and therefore under different settlements. The family history of the Bowers of Welham, merchants, bankers and landowners[223], illustrates some of these complexities in a small estate which covered about 2000 acres in the 1870s. There were related families of Bowers at Newcastle and in the North and East Riding. These different family lands had become concentrated in the family of Bower of Welham by the beginning of the nineteenth century.

Robert Bower, merchant of Newcastle upon Tyne, by his will of 1691 left his land (subject to his wife's dower rights) to his elder son John in tail general (i.e. including both males and females) with remainder to his younger son William in tail general. John Bower had no children, so that on his death in 1710 the inheritance passed under his father's will to the younger son, William Bower of Malton. In 1716 William docked the entail and held the lands in fee simple until 1777 when at his death his lands passed by his will to his cousin John Bower of Scorton (1730–1797) as a fee simple.

John Bower of Scorton was already heir to his own father Leonard. Leonard had acquired his brother's lands to enable him to make a marriage settlement, and the articles of his marriage settlement had bound him to provide a jointure and to settle one manor on his eldest son, in tail male, but had allowed him to revoke other parts of the entail as he wished. He died in 1765 leaving his unsettled lands to his second but only surviving son John. From 1765 to 1797 John Bower appears to have held his lands in fee simple, subject only to a charge on £150 worth of lands to assure his wife's jointure.

Another inheritance came to the Bowers: John of Scorton's youngest son Robert (1769–1835) inherited the estate of Welham in 1777 from his grandfather's half-brother, who had bought it in the 1750s. Welham was strictly settled on Robert in tail male, with remainders over. The intention was that Welham would provide a separate estate for a younger son: but as Robert's two eldest brothers died in their father's lifetime without children, it was Robert who in 1797 possessed all the lands described above, inherited from different family sources. Some were held in fee simple, some were entailed. Robert's articles of agreement on marriage in 1789 did not settle the estate held in fee simple, merely promised within six years to settle an estate of £300 to assure a jointure of £200. Robert Bower held the estates until his death in 1835. His son and heir came of age in 1819, but ways of disentailing the settled parts of the estate were under discussion as early as 1809. In 1835 Robert Bower's short and simple will, after making minor bequests to his four other children, left all his property to his son Robert Bower (1798–1869) and his heirs 'for ever', that is, in fee simple. He too was followed by another Robert Bower (1832–1886) who likewise, by a will which was proved in 1869, inherited the estates in fee simple. This family reversed the apparent trend among landowners towards more continuous settlement, by leaving their land deliberately unsettled for most of the nineteenth century. This was possibly because the Bowers held only a small estate, and also had commercial interests.

(vi) *The Lowthers (earls of Lonsdale)*

The Lowthers of Cumberland and Westmorland became by the 1750s one of the richest of English landowning families; their wealth was sustained throughout their rise in the peerage, and in 1883 the head of the family, the 5th earl of Lonsdale, held 68,000 acres[224]. Their family history was such that the possessions of different branches of the family (Lowthers of Lowther, of Whitehaven and of Maulds Meaburn) came together in the middle of the eighteenth century to enrich the 1st earl of Lonsdale and his successors[225].

The Lowthers of Lowther should be accounted the senior branch of the family, with land in four northern counties. They acquired first a baronetcy and then (in 1696) the title of baron Lowther of Lowther and viscount Lonsdale. Sir John Lowther of Lowther (1655–1700), 1st viscount, made his final will in 1698[226]. After making various bequests he strictly settled his estates 'to the Intent and Purpose that all and singular my reall Estate whatsoever may be remain and continue so long as it shall please Almighty God in my Name and Blood and may be enjoyed whole and intire' on his first son for life and on his issue male, remainder to his second son for life and his issue male, remainders to those specified in his marriage settlement of 1674. His marriage settlement, made by his grandfather when John was under age, had settled the jointure estates and fixed the size of portions and entailed all the other estates, subject however to a power of revocation and new appointment reserved to the settlor; but it appears that by the time of his last will Sir John held his lands in fee simple, probably from his coming of age in 1676 (he had inherited from his grandfather in 1675)[227]. In his will he copied the order of entail of 1674, substituting life tenancies for his sons in place of tenancies in tail, and not bothering to repeat the list of more distant heirs set out for the jointure lands in 1674 but merely referring to that order as already established. Perhaps with three sons he felt it unlikely that his direct line would die out. His optimism was misplaced.

Two of the sons of Sir John, the 1st viscount Lonsdale, succeeded in turn, in 1700 and 1713 (the third son died before he could inherit). They succeeded as minors, and even when they had come of age, under their father's will they were still limited to life tenancies. As neither married, there was no son with which either of them could break the entail, and in 1751, on the death of the 3rd viscount, the estates passed, as had been laid down in 1674 and 1698, to a great nephew and cousin, Sir James Lowther, of the junior branch of Lowther of Maulds Meaburn, who now became tenant in tail of the Lowther estates and subsequently became the 1st earl of Lonsdale[228].

Another member of the Lowther clan, Sir John Lowther of Whitehaven (1642–1706) had held his Whitehaven estates as a fee simple from c.1660 to 1701. In 1701 he made a strict settlement not on his elder son but on his younger son James, giving him a life estate, in tail male, with remainders to the three sons of the 1st viscount Lonsdale in tail male, and to the other branches of the Lowther family, and in the last resort the final remainder would go to Sir John's elder son[229]. But the strict settlement of 1701 contained a general power, enabling Sir John to revoke the settlement, and he chose to exercise this power in his last will of 1705, the last of his three surviving wills[230], substituting instead of the life tenancy that James would have received a much less restricted grant of the estate to James 'and his heirs male lawfully begotten'. As Sir John also revoked the appointment (made in the 1701 deed) of trustees to preserve the contingent remainders, James, who had no sons, could, and did, acquire the fee simple of the estates by a legal process after his father's death. Sir John explained in his will that he was altering the arrangements because James needed more powers than a life tenancy would give him, to manage the collieries and other business interests, and 'it doth not seem reasonable to lay him in whose conduct I have perfect confidençe under greater restraints that those yet unborne of whose dispositions wee can have no foresight'[231].

Sir John Lowther of Whitehaven died in 1706 and in January 1707 his younger son James completed the legal process of obtaining the fee simple of the estates by suffering a common recovery[232]. He kept the estates unsettled for nearly fifty years until his death, when still unmarried, in 1755. Sir James had made his last will in September 1754. He was seised in fee of a large real estate and also leasehold properties held under sixteen different leases. By his will he divided his estates between two of his cousins, both in different branches of the family. He settled the estates strictly: the greater part, his property in Cumberland[233], went to his cousin Sir William Lowther of Holker and Marske for life in tail male, with remainder to another cousin Sir James Lowther of Maulds Meaburn[234], the future 1st earl of Lonsdale, in tail male, with remainders over to other Lowthers. Sir James Lowther of Maulds Meaburn was left the Westmorland lands and an estate in Middlesex and Surrey in fee simple, together with a considerable amount of shares and money. The will went on to state, rather as Sir John's will had stated in 1705, that the Cumberland estate required great application and care in management, and therefore the testator did not want to divide it. He tried to arrange that Sir William Lowther of Holker and Marske would give Sir James Lowther of Maulds Meaburn all his Yorkshire land, and Sir James would give Sir William all his Cumberland land, as soon as Sir James came of age. The inducement to the two men was a trust fund set up by the same will, of £30,000 of South Sea Company annuities, a fund which was to be divided between the two men if the exchanges were made, but would go to one only if the other refused to exchange[235].

On Sir William's death unmarried in 1756, the Whitehaven estates passed under the entail to Sir James to add to those he had inherited already (see table, pp.76–7, a simplified family tree which it is hoped may make clear the transfer of property between various Lowthers called Sir John, Sir William and Sir James)[236]. Sir William Lowther had only lived long enough to hold the Whitehaven estates for thirteen months, and during that time Sir James was still under age, so it had not been practicable to make the exchange of estates. Subsequently a Chancery case was brought by Lord Charles Cavendish, executor and residuary legatee of Sir William, who failed in his suit to obtain either the South Sea stock of the trust fund or some Cumberland leasehold property which he alleged had not been included in the devise[237].

The Lowther families

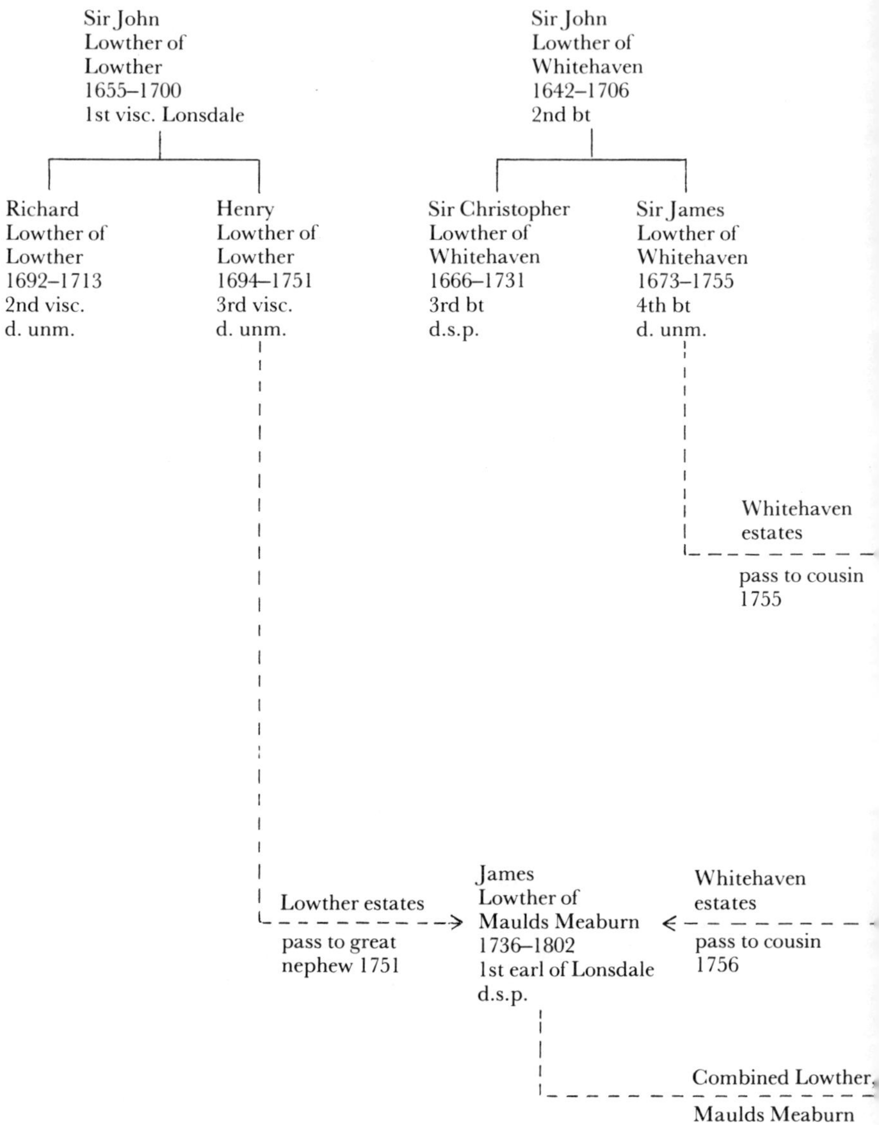

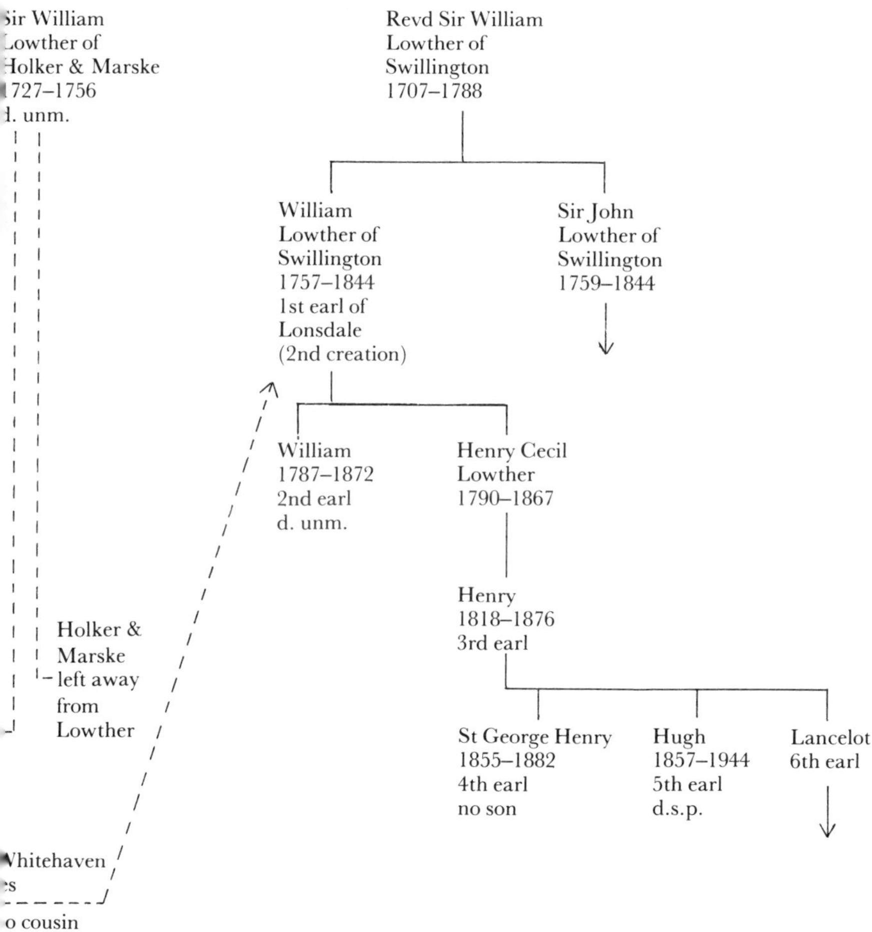
Sir William Lowther of Holker & Marske 1727–1756 d. unm.
Revd Sir William Lowther of Swillington 1707–1788
William Lowther of Swillington 1757–1844 1st earl of Lonsdale (2nd creation)
Sir John Lowther of Swillington 1759–1844
William 1787–1872 2nd earl d. unm.
Henry Cecil Lowther 1790–1867
Henry 1818–1876 3rd earl
Holker & Marske left away from Lowther
St George Henry 1855–1882 4th earl no son
Hugh 1857–1944 5th earl d.s.p.
Lancelot 6th earl
Whitehaven
o cousin

Sir James Lowther of Maulds Meaburn, 1st earl of Lonsdale (1736–1802), had now acquired the valuable estates of three branches of the family, although he was still under age. He had begun his life as a second son of a minor branch of the family, but outlived his elder brother and inherited the family estates in Maulds Meaburn in Westmorland and elsewhere in 1745. He also succeeded to the baronetcy and the Lowther of Lowther estates in March 1751 by his great-uncle's death without heirs, as tenant in tail of the will proved in 1700; and in 1755 and 1756 as life tenant to the Whitehaven estates and a large fortune under the will of his distant cousin Sir James Lowther of Whitehaven[238]. He was a notorious character of great wealth and bad reputation. During his life he acquired three baronies, two viscountcies and an earldom, and a further barony and viscountcy in 1797, the patent of 1797 including a special remainder of these titles (as he had no sons) to the male heirs of the body of his cousin the Revd Sir William Lowther of Swillington. On the earl's death in 1802, his will divided his property, devising the Yorkshire estate in strict settlement to his cousin John Lowther, and his own branch of the family's estate in Barbados to his sisters. However the greater part of the inheritance, the Cumberland and Westmorland estates of Lowther and Maulds Meaburn, was strictly settled by the earl's will on his cousin Sir William Lowther of Swillington, on whom the Whitehaven estates had already been entailed under the will proved in 1755, should the male lines of Lowther of Holker and Marske and of Maulds Meaburn fail, as had now happened[239].

The Lowthers of Swillington held lands mainly in the West Riding of Yorkshire. The Revd William Lowther, son of an eighth son, had unexpectedly inherited the estate of his cousin Sir William Lowther of Swillington in 1763, all the seven elder sons having no surviving male issue. The lands were strictly settled, or, as he wrote in his will 'entailed upon me for life, and after my decease on my issue male, and on failure of such to others in remainder, and it being in my Power jointly with my eldest son when he came of age [which was in 1778] by the advice and opinion of Counsel learned in the Law to dock the said Entail, it was accordingly done and settled to other uses . . .'[240]. He was granted a baronetcy in 1764: as the Revd Sir William

Lowther Bt he made his will in 1787, during the lifetime of James Lowther, 1st earl of Lonsdale, at a time when he was aware that he and his sons were next in the entail established by Lowther of Whitehaven in 1755, and would therefore inherit unless the 1st earl had a son. With this in mind, Lowther of Swillington settled the greater part of his property in the West Riding on his eldest son William for life and his son's male issue, with some West and East Riding lands going to his younger son John and his issue male, with cross remainders (i.e. William's line would inherit if John's line died out and vice versa) and other remainders over. But he added a proviso that if his son William or his issue male inherited the Whitehaven estates under the 1755 will of Sir James Lowther, then the dispositions he was making in 1787 would be void, and the younger branch of the family (John and his issue) would inherit all the Yorkshire lands, strictly settled. This in fact happened: when William, son of the Revd Sir William, inherited the Whitehaven estates in 1802, his younger brother John and his descendants gained the Yorkshire lands[241].

William Lowther (1757–1844), the fortunate heir to the different estates the Lowthers had held in the north west, became in 1802 tenant for life of his cousin's aggregation of the estates of Lowther and Maulds Meaburn, and tenant in tail of the Whitehaven estates. He also succeeded as viscount and baron Lowther, and was in addition made 1st earl of Lonsdale (of the 2nd creation) in 1807. His son (also called William) came of age in 1808, and it seems likely that about that time father and son disentailed, and left the estates unsettled: they were certainly unsettled at William Lowther's death in 1844[242]. His will made a new settlement. He left all his estates in the counties of York, Cumberland and Westmorland to trustees, for the use of eight named male relatives and their issue male successively, the named men to be tenants for life and their issue tenants in tail. But the whole of the strict settlement was subject to a general power of appointment to be exercised jointly by the 1st earl's two sons: they could 'revoke alter or vary all or any of the trusts . . . limit appoint and declare . . . such new or modified trusts . . . as my said sons shall concur in thinking fit and expedient for any family arrangements or settlement or any other purpose whatsoever'. In default of such appointment the strict settlement would stand[243].

The 1844 settlement lasted for eleven years: in January 1855 the two brothers combined to exercise their power and again settled the estate strictly, following the same entail, which in both 1844 and 1855 created a life tenancy for the 2nd earl with remainder to his issue male, and in the event of the 2nd earl having no issue male, a life tenancy for his brother Henry Cecil Lowther, a further life tenancy to Henry Cecil Lowther's son Henry Lowther, with remainder to his first and other sons in tail male with remainders over[244]. The 2nd earl died unmarried in 1872, and as he had outlived his brother, the settled estates passed under the 1855 settlement to his nephew Henry Lowther, who became the 3rd earl and life tenant of the Lonsdale estates.

Henry Lowther, 3rd earl of Lonsdale, made his will shortly before he died in 1876. At that time the estates were still settled under the 1855 deed, and the third earl in his will requested that any tenant in tail who might inherit should within six months (or within six months of becoming 21) disentail and resettle, the terms of the new settlement being laid down in the will, naming a succession of five remaindermen and their issue male, and including a clause that any one born in the testator's lifetime was to be a life tenant only. Within two months of the 3rd earl's death his son St George Henry Lowther, the 4th earl, came of age and as tenant in tail in possession under the 1855 settlement immediately disentailed and resettled in accordance with his father's will. On marriage in 1878 the 4th earl charged the estates with pin-money, portions and jointure. When, in 1880, the 4th earl obtained a private act of Parliament to enable him to raise money to buy coal mines in Cumbria, the act included a précis of the 1876 entail set out as follows:

> Persons living in 1880 entitled to the settled estates in succession: the 4th earl being tenant for life and also entitled to the ultimate reversion, and each of the others being tenant for life in remainder:
>
> The 4th earl of Lonsdale
> Hugh Cecil Lowther
> Charles Edwin Lowther } younger sons of the 3rd earl
> Lancelot Edward Lowther

William Lowther	brother of the 3rd earl
James William Lowther Gerard Augustus Lowther Harold Arthur Lowther Henry Cecil Lowther the younger	sons of William Lowther & nephews of the 3rd earl

Persons unborn in 1880 who might become entitled to the settled estates:

Issue male of the 4th earl
Issue male of Hugh Cecil Lowther
Issue male of Charles Edwin Lowther
Issue male of Lancelot Edward Lowther
Issue male of James William Lowther
Issue male of Gerard Augustus Lowther
Issue male of Harold Arthur Lowther
Issue male of Henry Cecil Lowther the younger
Sons born after 1880 to William Lowther and their issues male[245]

In the event the 4th earl died in 1882 leaving one daughter, and was succeeded by his next brother Hugh Cecil Lowther as 5th earl of Lonsdale.

Hugh Lowther the 5th earl (1857–1944) grew up as a second son, not expecting to inherit the earldom and the estates, and perpetually short of money. Two years before he inherited, as next heir to his brother, he sold his contingent reversionary interest in the 68,000 acre Lowther estates to a money lender for the paltry sum of £40,000[246]. The reversion was repurchased from the money lender by the trustees of the 1876 settlement. When the 4th earl unexpectedly died in 1882, Hugh Lowther should have become the next life tenant, enjoying all the estate revenues and, within the limits of the settlement, possessed of considerable powers. But because he had sold his life interest, he found the trustees were in command of the estates and so collected the income. For as long as Hugh Lowther lived, his (never-to-be-born) son was hypothetically the next in the entail, so that Hugh Lowther could not be replaced in the estates by the succession of his brother (who eventually became the 6th earl when Hugh died without a son in 1944). So by selling his life interest he did not lose everything. He was also the 5th earl of Lonsdale, a dignity which the trustees wished to maintain. The trustees (the senior man was a Lowther cousin) made him a substantial annual allowance (about £80,000) and for the rest of his long life he continued to enjoy all the Lowther properties as 'the Yellow Earl'. But he was always something less than a life tenant, 'a sort of pensioner on the estates' constantly at odds with his trustees over the size of his allowance[247].

Lowther of Lowther

1674–1676	settled at marriage subject to general power
1676?	disentailed?
1676?–1700	unsettled
1700–1751	strictly settled by will proved 1700
1751–1802	unsettled? Held by tenant in tail

Lowther of Whitehaven

c.1660–1701	unsettled
1701–1706	settled subject to general power
1706–1707	settlement revoked by exercise of power by will and subsequent recovery of 1707
1707–1755	unsettled
1755–1802	strictly settled by will proved 1755

Lowther earls of Lonsdale (Lowther, Whitehaven, Maulds Meaburn)

1802–1808?	strictly settled by will proved 1802
1808–1844	unsettled
1844–1855	settled subject to general power
1855–1876	strictly settled by exercise of power by deed
1876–1944	strictly settled by disentailing and resettlement of 1876

(vii) *The Dawnay family (viscounts Downe)*

The Dawnay family hold the Irish viscountcy of Downe, acquired in

1681. Their seventeenth-century estates were centred on Cowick near Selby, Sessay near Thirsk, and Danby in Yorkshire. Later acquisitions were the Wykeham estate near Scarborough and Baldersby Park near Thirsk[248]. The family owned about 38,000 Yorkshire acres in 1875, divided between the dowager viscountess Downe and her son: the dowager having the larger share[249].

The first viscount Downe was twice married, and was succeeded in 1690 by his sixth but eldest surviving son Henry, who became the 2nd viscount and died in 1741. Settlements made by the 1st and 2nd viscounts have not been found. The 2nd viscount outlived his son and was succeeded by his grandson, Henry Pleydell Dawnay, who was born in 1727. On his coming of age the 3rd viscount disentailed the estates and for the rest of his life (he died unmarried in 1760) enjoyed the fee simple. He was succeeded by his brother as 4th viscount, who made a post-nuptial settlement on his wife four years after the articles of agreement had been drawn up in 1763. The 4th viscount was succeeded in turn by his two sons, the 5th viscount (1764–1832) who had no children, and the Revd William Henry Dawnay, 6th viscount (1772–1846) whose direct descendants held the estates into the twentieth century.

Settlement history of the Dawnay family (viscounts Downe)

1660–1749	not known
1749–1767	fee simple after disentailing by tenant in tail in possession
1767–1819	strictly settled by post-nuptial settlement
1819–1832	settled subject to a general power of appointment
1832–1843	strictly settled by will made 1819, proved 1832
1843–1846	base fee established by disentailing of 1843
1846–1849	fee simple established by further disentailing of 1846
1849–1865	strictly settled by post-nuptial settlement
1865–1893	disentailed and strictly settled on heir's majority
1893–	settled subject to joint general powers of appointment

There are some unusual features in the Downe settlements. The establishment of a base fee in 1843 is remarkable: it was achieved by the heir and his younger (and only) brother barring their own successors, but it did not create a fee simple because their father, the 6th viscount and life tenant, did not participate. The father may simply have refused, or he may have been mentally incapable: the archives do not reveal. The manoeuvre seems to have been designed to facilitate the marriage settlement of the heir, as the heir's brother undertook to provide the jointure if necessary. On the father's death, the base fee was easily destroyed, and the fee simple established.

In the post-nuptial settlements of 1767 and 1849, the heirs to the estates had already been born, and the boys were not made tenants for life of the estates, but were designated as tenants in tail. This is unlike the pattern of most of the other great estates investigated: families like the Constables (see below, p.85) (who in the late eighteenth century were consulting the same London conveyancers over their settlements as the Downes) carried the settlement as far into the future as possible. In 1893 the Dawnay heir was made life tenant only, but as he and his father were in possession of joint general powers (and after the father's death, the heir and his brother could exercise the power) they were not restricted in their actions.

In 1851 the Dawnays inherited East Riding lands from Richard Langley, a cousin, owner of Wykeham Abbey, who died without any children in 1817. Langley had settled his estates on Marmaduke Dawnay, a younger son of the 4th viscount Downe, on condition he changed his name to Langley. When Marmaduke in his turn died unmarried in 1851, his nephew William Henry Dawnay, 7th viscount, inherited the estates under the 1817 will as tenant in tail. He disentailed and the Langley estates were not thereafter strictly settled, but settled subject to a general power. The settlement of the Wykeham Abbey estates in this period was as below:

Settlement history of the Wykeham Abbey estate, East Yorkshire

1660–1772	not traced
1772–1817	settled (according to private act of 1802) terms unknown
1817–1851	strictly settled by will proved 1817
1851–1857	fee simple after disentailing of 1851
1857–1900	settled by will proved 1857, subject to a general power of appointment

The large amount of land held by the dowager viscountess in 1875 was a combination of the Langley estates, which the 7th viscount had inherited, disentailed and left to his wife in 1857, and land he had bought and not settled during his life. He made arrangements in his will for the inheritance of this land, which he gave to his wife for her life only, but he also gave his wife a power of revocation (which she used) to alter any or all of his arrangements.

(viii) *Other families*

The remaining examples of family settlements are dealt with in less detail, as there are no new principles which emerge from the variety of settlement practice given above[250].

The title to the Constable estates at Burton Constable and elsewhere in East Yorkshire (amounting to 10,000 acres in 1883) was derived from royal letters patent of the mid sixteenth century. The family solicitors of 1790 knew that there had been an entail in the late seventeenth century, but they were unable to find documents relating to it[251]. The difficulty in tracing the settlement history of the estates at this period may have been due to evasive action taken by the recusant Constables to avoid the various economic hazards of seventeenth-century Catholicism; such action as the deed of 1663 by which the viscount gave all his estates to trustees for 21 years (if he should live so long) for specified uses including maintenance of the viscount (Dunbar) and his wife, and the raising of portions for the children[252]. Although there were difficulties in deducing the seventeenth-century settlements, the lawyers of 1790 traced a continuous verifiable title from 1717. From that date the settlement pattern continued:

Settlement history of the Constables of Burton Constable, East Yorkshire

1666–1717	settled (deed unknown)
1717–1747	strictly settled by will proved 1717
1747–1791	fee simple after disentailing by tenant in tail in possession
1791–1827	strictly settled by will proved 1791
1827–1870	settled after disentailing by tenant in tail in possession, subject to general power of appointment
1870–1912	strictly settled by will proved 1870[253]

The descent of lands of the dukes of Newcastle was complicated by inheritance of land from several sources and partitions of the estates. In 1691 Henry, duke of Newcastle, by his will devised the Cavendish estates to one of his daughters, in strict settlement, on the two conditions that the heir to the estates must take the name of Cavendish, and that the estates must not be divided. This daughter was married to John Holles, earl of Clare, later duke of Newcastle, who in addition to the life interest in his wife's Cavendish lands inherited additional Holles estates from a second cousin. John Holles by his will proved in 1711, split the estates, some going to his daughter but most to his nephew, Thomas Pelham, later duke of Newcastle. Subsequent dukes of Newcastle succeeded in keeping most of the Holles estates with the dukedom, even though a shortage of direct male heirs meant that the title to the dukedom had to be recreated three times between 1690 and 1780. The settlements of the estates withstood the insolvency of the dukes in the late eighteenth and in the late nineteenth century. The Cavendish lands were awarded to the Harleys by a division of lands about 1719, and subsequently through another heiress passed to the Bentinck family (dukes of Portland). They were strictly settled by will in 1755; after 1785 the Cavendish lands descended with the estates to the Cavendish-Bentincks. The largest holdings of both families were in Nottinghamshire.

Settlement history of the dukes of Newcastle

1691–1711	Cavendish estates strictly settled by will proved 1691: Holles estates inherited 1689 and 1694
1711–1741	strictly settled by will proved 1711, reinforced by private act of Parliament of 1719. Life interest put in trust because of debts, 1721 and 1738
(Holles lands only)	
1741–1744	settled (after disentailing) subject to a power of revocation
1744–1806	strictly settled by 1741 settlement, power of revocation given up on marriage of heir
1807–1832	strictly settled by marriage settlement after disentailing of 1806

1832–1856?	strictly settled by marriage settlement of 1832 (divorce 1850)
1856–1885	strictly settled by deed of 1856[254]

A complicated genealogical pattern of succession in the family of Willoughby (in 1712 granted the barony of Middleton) was followed by a settlement pattern that kept the family estates in Nottinghamshire, Yorkshire, Lincolnshire and Scotland together, although at different times some parts of the estates were settled with different remainders. Lord Middleton held 99,576 acres in 1883, of which two-thirds were in Ross-shire.

Settlement history of the Willoughbys (barons Middleton)

1677–1688	settled (terms unknown)
1694–c.1747	strictly settled by marriage settlement of 1694
c.1747–1758	position unknown (disentailing possible from 1747)
1758–1800	unsettled (successive wills of 1758, 1774 and 1781 devised unsettled estates)
1800–1848	Notts. estates strictly settled (after disentailing of 1848) by deed of 1848 and will made 1848 which came into effect 1857. (Yorks., Lincs. and Scottish estates settled differently)[255]

2 Families that failed

Chief Justice Crew, giving judgment in 1626 in favour of de Vere's claim to the earldom of Oxford, lamented the disappearance of some of the greatest names of the English Middle Ages in the phrases 'For where is Bohun? Where's Mowbray? Where's Mortimer? Nay, which is more, and most of all, where is Plantagenet?'[256]. These historic names had been lost: and if there were descendants of these families, they came through female lines. In the early eighteenth century this was amended by making fashionable the 'name and arms' clause in settlements, whereby a condition of succession was that the successor take the name and arms of a particular family. Such a clause ensured that the dukes of Northumberland were called Percy and not Smithson, the dukes of Marlborough continued to be Churchills and not Spencers, the owners of Holkham were Coke and not Roberts. It was ancient names that Crew spoke of in his judgement: ancient estates were a different problem. As we shall continue to demonstrate, family estates of the greater landowners had an excellent chance of survival in the era of strict settlement. Under complicated entails, even if the direct male line died out, the estates would continue in collateral lines, and names were changed or added to, in order that the 'name and blood' of the original owner might continue.

Until about the time of the Restoration of 1660 great estates could be dissipated by their owners, or confiscated by the state. After the Restoration it was rare for landed families to reach final ruin, that is, to lose all their land. Burke, in his account of the fall of families over the centuries, offers two causes: the law of attainder (which was very rarely invoked in the modern period) and 'the power vested in the heir of some one generation or another of alienating the whole hereditary estates of his family'[257]. This second reason was much the more significant after 1660: attainder affected some Irish and Scottish families, but virtually no English ones. Alienation (or the process of transferring the estates to someone outside the family) was only possible in the case of estates that were for some reason unsettled. Alienation was occasionally because of a whim, but more often the result of debts.

The problem of aristocratic indebtedness has been of interest both to nineteenth-century social critics and to twentieth-century historians. From the early seventeenth century through the eighteenth century to the late nineteenth century (and probably beyond) debt was a constant feature of life for the aristocracy[258]. Borrowing by landowners was often necessary to reconcile the fluctuations of income and expenditure, and even in times of stable or rising rents, various forms of extravagance, such as house building, elections, and buying and improving land could absorb more than the estates' income over a given period. During the eighteenth century various improvements in the credit field made it easier to borrow money[259]. Improvident heirs or wives, borrowing on their expectations or their husbands' legal liability to pay, could run up debts at prohibitive rates of interest. Estates could become encumbered in other ways: generous ancestors, for instance, could load the estates with portions and jointures. Large debts could be carried by landed estates for very long periods: but at some point the credit would fail, and when the creditors tried to recover their money, what recourse did they have against the strictly settled lands?

A man might have three kinds of debts: personal debts (such as notes of hand and household bills), bond debts, and mortgages. All these kinds of debt could be contracted by anyone, including life tenants and remaindermen, but the only kind that could affect the settled estates was the mortgage, and that only in certain circumstances.

Personal debts were not recoverable by the creditor from the settled estates, but only from the personal effects of the debtor. So if a life tenant's personal effects were insufficient, the unfortunate creditor or tradesman had no redress unless the next life tenant, or some relation concerned about the family name, chose to 'honour the debts', as the third marquis of Downshire did in 1809 when he volunteered to pay the personal debts of his dead father and grandfather[260].

Bonds were a common way of raising money. A man would borrow £1000 from, for instance, his solicitor: the only security would be that he bound himself to repay £1000 and a certain rate of interest before a particular date, and if he did not pay at the right time, he would owe £2000. Bonds almost invariably carried a penalty of twice the borrowed sum. If when the time for repayment came the debtor had no money available, he would take out another bond. A particular temptation to heirs to settled estates was to give post-obit bonds ('after he has died' bonds), a promise to repay a sum in the future, on coming into their inheritance, as their eventual succession was assured by the settlement[261]. Provided the heir was young and healthy, and likely to inherit before too long, lending him money was a reasonable risk. Bonds, even post-obit bonds, were still personal debts and could not be claimed against the settled estates.

The settled estates were often liable for annuities or rent charges paid from the estate income, usually to relatives and almost always to widows. Such payments could be enforced by the recipient through the power of distraint written into the settlement[262]. Sometimes the life tenant, unable to mortgage the estates himself (because he did not have the appropriate power) mortgaged his own life interest, in which case the mortgage was often protected by a life insurance policy, with the premiums secured on the estate income. Sometimes the heir, knowing that he must inherit under the strict settlement should he live long enough, could mortgage his own reversionary interest. The duke of Buckingham's debts before 1845 were mainly on the security of his life interest (and before he had succeeded he had borrowed on his reversionary interest) and his life was insured for nearly £300,000 to protect these loans[263]. The heir to the Lonsdale estates sold his reversionary interest (above, pp.81–2).

Through a combination of any or all of household bills, bond debts and mortgages on the life interest, a man could become personally insolvent. A personal disaster could, however, leave the settled land untouched; this after all was one of the motives for making strict settlements. In 1870, when the duke of Newcastle became bankrupt[264], he gave up his life interest in the estates, and the bailiffs moved into his houses. The estate income went to his creditors, as long as that duke lived. But on his death, the settled estates and the heirlooms (mainly in Clumber) passed to the heir, freed from his predecessor's personal debts[265].

Mortgages of the fee simple came into a different category. In the interval after a former settlement was ended, and before resettlement took place (an interval which might be minutes, hours, days or years) the unsettled land (the 'fee simple') could be charged with mortgages, as it was in the Buckingham family in 1845 and the Sykes settlement of 1900[266]. The land could at that time also be charged with potential future mortgages, such as provision to raise capital sums for unborn children, which might never be needed; but the opportunity was taken, while the land was out of settlement, to create powers so that the trustees and the life tenant could, in certain circumstances in future, mortgage the fee simple of the estates. Once resettlement had taken place, the fee simple went into suspension, unavailable to the trustees and life tenants until the next disentailing, but still carrying any mortgages laid on it while it was unsettled, and capable of carrying potential mortgages that could be made under appropriate powers. Such powers were normally restricted to particular purposes, and almost invariably specified the largest amount that could be raised: for instance, a common reason for a power of mortgaging was to provide portions for the younger children, and the ceiling on portions would be written into the settlement[267].

Many great estates carried mortgages for decades, transferring them sometimes from one mortgagee to another. The mortgagees would often be relatives and friends, as well as lawyers and insurance companies[268]. In some cases mortgages on the fee simple could be held by the life tenant himself (as happened in the Sykes family in the late nineteenth and early twentieth centuries)[269] or, as on the Middleton estates, some of the mortgage money raised under the family settlement of 1876 was borrowed from the trustees of the 1848 settlement: one part of the estate borrowing from the other[270]. In such cases the mortgagees were not likely to press for repayment. A first mortgage on landed property was considered an excellent investment, and was not likely to be called in so long as the estate appeared solvent: if the mortgagees wished to recover their loan, then the mortgage could usually be transferred elsewhere. Sometimes the mortgagee would actually try to avoid having the mortgage paid off, for, as Mrs Arnold told the House of Lords in 1717, 'stocks were now very high and she could not lay out her money to so good advantage as it was upon the mortgage, which is at 6 per cent'[271].

It was only difficulties with the mortgages of the estates themselves, that is, of the fee simple, that could cause disruption to the settled lands. At the approach of such a disaster, the first step in a crisis was often to assign the settled estates temporarily to a new group of trustees, who would reduce the tangled affairs of the estates to order, by consolidating debts, raising rents, realising the available resources, and urging the life tenant to simplify his lifestyle. This was the course taken by the duke of Newcastle in both 1721 and 1738, earl Grosvenor in 1779, Lord Verney in 1780 and the marquis of Ailesbury in 1832[272]. The family would avoid selling land as long as possible: 'bitterly unpalatable, it would be resorted to only in the severest adversity'[273]. But if the trusteeship failed, it might be necessary to obtain a private act of Parliament, to break the settlement and allow the sale of part of the estates to redeem the overwhelming debts. The power to sell for this purpose was a common ground for obtaining a private act[274].

The ultimate collapse might come if the life tenant, using the estate income for his own purposes, failed to pay the interest charges on the mortgages of the fee simple of the estate. In some cases accumulated charges meant that the interest due actually exceeded the income of the estate. Then there was a serious risk of the mortgagees (particularly if they were not relatives or friends) selling up the estate. Most mortgages of a fee simple allowed the mortgagees to sell the land to recover their loan, if the debt was not paid off when asked for, or if the interest fell into long overdue arrears. Without such a power of sale, the mortgagees had to follow a slow and expensive process of foreclosure.

The Verneys of Claydon overreached their resources in the later eighteenth century, through a mixture of personal extravagance, election expenses and the attempt to build a house to rival the Buckingham family's Stowe. In the 1780s the estate was in the hands of trustees, but the debts still pressed. In 1790 the bailiffs were in the house, and eventually all the contents (except the pictures, which were heirlooms) were sold: it was said that Lord Verney only escaped his creditors by leaving the house in his wife's hearse. Nevertheless although lands were subsequently sold, Claydon as an estate survived the personal ruin of Lord Verney, and is still the home of the Verney family[275]. The Myddelton family of Chirk Castle managed to keep afloat on a sea of debts from c.1718 into the next century: lurching from one-expedient to another, through trusts and through disentailing. Eventually large areas of land were sold, but the family never lost everything, and remained landed gentry in possession of Chirk Castle into the twentieth century[276]. Similarly the sale of the duke of Chandos's Canons in 1744 and William Beckford's Fonthill in 1822 (both as the result of debts) did not leave either family landless or penniless.

As has already been noted above (p.12), it is much easier to find the settlements of successful families (in this context, those that survived with some landed property into the twentieth century) than those that were completely ruined. The archives of a family like that of Sir Thomas Conyers, who died around 1810, as a pauper in the workhouse, and whose three daughters married working men, are obviously less likely to be in a muniment room than those of the dukes of Devonshire[277]. It is, however, possible to trace, at least in outline, the settlement history of some families that failed.

(i) *The Herons of Chipchase*

The Herons of Chipchase, Northumberland, are one example of a great landowning family who lost all their estates and became penniless. The history of their decline can be traced from printed genealogical sources, a Chancery case, and two private acts of Parliament[278].

The Heron family had acquired Chipchase in the fourteenth century by marriage and owned widespread lands around Hadrian's Wall, producing in 1647 an income of about £1200 per annum. On 1 January 1647 two settlements were made of all the Heron lands, including the castles of Sewingshields and Simonburn and nine other manors, which had previously been held in fee simple. Four-fifths of the estate was settled on the owner Cuthbert Heron senior for life, with remainder to his son (also Cuthbert Heron) in tail male, remainder to his son's daughters and further remainders to seven other named Herons in tail male. By the second settlement, one-fifth of the estate, worth £240 a year, was immediately settled on the marriage of the heir to provide his maintenance and a jointure for his widow if necessary.

In 1655 Cuthbert Heron senior died, and his son Cuthbert became tenant for life. In 1662 he was made a baronet. Sir Cuthbert Heron was already in financial difficulties by 1669, when he owed a 'great debt' of some £4000, because of his imprisonment and other troubles 'in the late unhappy tymes' and also 'some great and expensive suits at lawe', together with his purchase of a rent charge his father had laid on the estates for Cuthbert senior's widow and daughter[279]. As well as his debt, Sir Cuthbert Heron had seven younger children for whom no provision had been made in the 1647 settlement, his wife's jointure was not valid against his heir (because although the two settlements had been made on the same day in 1647, Sir Cuthbert's marriage settlement had been executed after the settlement entailing the lands), nor could he jointure any future wife of his son. The combination led to a private act in 1669, whereby some land worth

£400 a year was vested in trustees, to be sold, mortgaged or leased, to raise £4000 for the debts and a maximum of £500 each for the younger children. Sir Cuthbert was also given power by the act to secure jointures for his own and his son's future wife[280]. By this 1669 act, presuming the land values had stayed the same since 1647, Sir Cuthbert had obtained the right to dispose of one quarter of the family's lands. He proceeded to mortgage lands, but both he and his successors were dilatory in paying the interest, so that there were 'great arrearages'.

In 1673 Sir Cuthbert's son came of age, and in 1675 father and son disentailed the estates, breaking the 1647 settlement, and then they resettled them. As in 1647 the estates were divided, most going to the father for life, and then entailed successively on his sons, but part being settled on the marriage of the eldest son, with the same entail. The eldest son married but died in his father's lifetime, leaving a daughter who under her father's marriage settlement was entitled to have £80 a year maintenance and £2500 portion. All the estates eventually came to the 2nd son of Sir Cuthbert, Sir John Heron, 2nd Bt. He did not pay his niece's money, and for that reason became involved in a Chancery dispute with the trustees. Chancery decreed a new settlement of part of the lands, in 1687, but the rest of the estate (at some time after 1688) was disentailed by Sir John as tenant in tail of the 1675 settlement[281] and remained unsettled until 1692.

In 1692 and 1693 by deed and by will Sir John settled the estates once more, and again as in 1669 part of the land was put in trust to be sold, mortgaged or leased. The land not so dealt with was entailed on his younger brother Charles, in tail male, with remainders to three other named Herons in tail male. The estates were additionally charged with payments to Sir John's daughter, his niece, four sisters and three dowagers. Sir Charles Heron, 3rd Bt, on succeeding his brother in 1693 to a decreased but heavily encumbered estate, found that his predecessors had contracted debts of £8000 and were involved in 'several great and expensive suits in law and equity' but as life tenant Sir Charles could not sell land to clear the debts, settle the law suits, raise the portions or pay the maintenance of the women. He obtained a private act in 1695 to enable further parts of the estate to be sold[282], to which the existing mortgagees' consent had to be given, but owing to the reluctance of buyers to acquire such heavily encumbered land, no sale was achieved until 1713, when finally after the intervention of the Master of the Rolls almost all the estates were sold[283].

Sir Charles Heron died c.1718. His son Sir Harry Heron, 4th Bt, found that all that was left of 'the vast estates of his ancestors'[284] was Chipchase itself, which he mortgaged in 1725. The mortgage money did not last long, and in 1727 Harry Heron sold Chipchase to the mortgagee, in return for a small sum of money and an annuity to Heron and his wife. Even the annuity was not safe, for in 1729 Heron mortgaged his annuity and then failed to pay the interest on that mortgage. He died in poverty in 1729.

The Heron family's difficulties apparently began in the Civil War. Their policy of obtaining private acts (in 1669 and 1695) or taking advantage of intervals in settlements in order to mortgage or sell the estates had not succeeded in restoring their position. Arrears of mortgage interest and arrears of maintenance and jointure payments meant that the indebtedness of the estate grew quickly. They were perhaps unfortunate in the number of women who had to be maintained by the estate, and they engaged in expensive law suits. Disposing of parts of the estate reduced the income: it did not seem to have alleviated the debt. Whereas many families in difficulties were saved by a good marriage, a fortunate inheritance or good management, the Herons were not.

Settlements of the Heron family of Chipchase

Before 1647	fee simple
1647–1675	settled by two deeds
1675–1688	settled after disentailing of 1675; confirmed by act of 1669
1688–1692	unsettled (but part settled by Chancery decree)
1692–1695	strictly settled by deed of 1692 and will of 1693
1695–1713	vested in trustees to be sold under act of 1695

Chipchase itself had several more changes of owner. It was sold by the purchasers of 1727 (who were also the mortgagees) to John Reed in 1734: he left it by will to his sister's second son Christopher, who changed his name to Reed. Christopher's son and heir John was a partner in a Newcastle bank that failed, and in 1823 he conveyed his estates to trustees for the uses of his creditors, with the concurrence of his son whose 'high sense of honour induced him to join his father in breaking the entail of Chipchase so that the estate might be sold to pay the creditors, conduct which was greatly extolled'[285]. The estate was subsequently sold twice more in the century. For both the Herons and the Reeds, the crucial event in losing the estates was the breaking of the settlement.

(ii) *The marquis of Ailesbury*

The estates of the marquis of Ailesbury have already been mentioned as an example of estates put into trust to cope with large debts (above, p.91). Although the trust of 1832 was not in this case particularly successful in reducing the debts, it avoided the necessity for sales of land. Later in the century disaster came closer to the Ailesburys.

In the 1880s the 3rd marquis was tenant for life of the Ailesbury properties at Savernake in Wiltshire and Jervaulx in Yorkshire. The heir to both and tenant in tail of the settlements was the 3rd marquis's grandson, Lord Savernake, who would eventually inherit a considerable amount of land as absolute owner. Unfortunately he was a very extravagant young man, and by the time he was 21 his debts had reached about £175,000, and on coming of age, he also converted his estates tail in both properties into base fees[286]. To pay his debts, his grandfather very reluctantly agreed to join with him in selling the Yorkshire estate, but insisted that if he did so, Lord Savernake would have to renew the entail of Savernake. An indenture of settlement was made in 1885, which strictly settled Savernake on Lord Savernake for his life, with remainder to his heirs male and various remainders over. The following year the 3rd marquis died, leaving the Savernake estate of some 40,000 acres duly entailed on his grandson.

Within a few years of inheriting the 4th marquis was ruined. He had mortgaged his own life interest to the extent of over £200,000, the principal mortgagee had brought an action for foreclosure, and a receiver had been appointed. A receiving order in bankruptcy had also been made against the marquis, but the proceedings had been suspended while the marquis tried to sell his estates. His gross annual rental was £27,000 but after paying outgoings, jointures (there were four dowagers to support) and other charges, the net annual income was only £900. In 1891 the marquis applied to Chancery for permission to sell the whole of the entailed estates, including the mansion house and park. Under the Settled Lands Acts of 1882 and 1890 he could sell agricultural land of his own volition, so long as the money raised remained subject to the settlement: but he could not sell the mansion house and park without the trustees' permission. One of the trustees, the 4th marquis's uncle and next heir, refused permission and in the courts eight remaindermen of the 1885 settlement, all Brudenell-Bruces, also objected. The case was heard in Chancery, went to the Court of Appeal and to the House of Lords (*re Marquis of Ailesbury's Settled Estates* and *Bruce* v. *Ailesbury*). The judgments described what the judges believed would happen if the estates were not sold: the tenant for life would be bankrupt and the money-lenders would put in a receiver to adminster the estate, who would for the rest of the marquis's life (for that would be the length of their tenure) extract every penny they could from it and leave it and everyone connected with it ruined. Although the marquis won the right to sell the estate, the case had taken so long that the prospective purchaser, Lord Iveagh, was no longer interested; but the 4th marquis died soon after, and his uncle, who succeeded under the 1884 settlement, gradually restored the estates, which remained intact until 1929[287].

(iii) *John Mytton of Halston*

Estates which were not settled were more easily sold or left away from the family than those estates which had to be freed from settlement. John Mytton (1796–1834) of Halston, Shropshire, succeeded as tenant in tail in possession to a landed property of about £10,000 a year. He was insanely extravagant and addicted to gambling and is alleged to have spent half a million pounds in fifteen years, his agent trying in vain to control him. In 1831 all his property was sold by his creditors, except for Halston itself which was entailed on his son by Mytton's marriage settlement. John Mytton died of delirium tremens in the King's Bench prison in 1834. His son, another John Mytton, also succeeded as tenant in tail and after his coming of age disposed of the remaining part of the once-great Halston estate[288].

(iv) *Lord Rancliffe*
The 2nd Lord Rancliffe of Bunny Hall, Nottinghamshire, acquired a fee simple of his estates by disentailing when he came of age, and, dying in 1850, left all his lands to his mistress absolutely, without trustees or any restriction on their future. Although in 1861 the will was contested by the heir at law, on the grounds of undue influence, it was not overturned, and the lady lived on until 1875 in possession of the estates, when she devised them by her will to a spinster niece; but, so strong was the tradition of 'Family' even in a mistress who had spent her life in quarrelling with the Rancliffe relatives, that she left the reversion of the estates after the end of her niece's life tenancy to a member of the Rancliffe family, who inherited in 1910 (and sold the estates)[289].

(v) *The duke of Buckingham*
The most famous nineteenth-century case of insolvency was that of the 2nd duke of Buckingham. He inherited encumbrances and mortgages and added to them considerably, both as heir and as life tenant. Some of the mortgages were on the settled estates (in accordance with the powers of previous settlements) but most were on the 2nd duke's life interest: by 1844 when his son Lord Chandos came of age the duke owed over £1 million. He and his son disentailed all the family estates available to them, and charged the estates, now unsettled, with a mortgage to pay off most of the duke's debts. But the whole process, hindered by the duke's obstinacy and chicanery, took too long. Resettlement was never achieved, because the duke refused to execute the documents[290]. By 1847 the annual charges on the estates exceeded income by more than £20,000. The mortgagees were left without interest, and, anxious to recover their money, they put the duke's mansion house, Stowe, and its contents up for sale in 1848. Thereafter the largest part of the estates, some 50,000 acres, were sold: only the Chandos property survived, about 10,000 acres that could not be disentailed until the next generation, being held under a different settlement.

The Times criticised the duke and his son Chandos for disentailing the greater part of the estates: if Chandos had refused, and merely waited for his father to die, most of the debts would have died with him. But Chandos would have no income, and the family would have had to endure creditors administering the estates, for as long as the 2nd duke lived: the situation foretold by the judges in the Ailesbury case[291]. Chandos's advisers expected a resettlement: but as this never happened, the disentailed estates were at the mercy of the creditors. Crashes such as Buckingham's were unusual: and even in that family, strict settlement preserved 10,000 acres[292]. In many families, debt forced sales of land (authorised through a private estate act, or, later in the nineteenth century, by general enabling acts) but total extinction of a settled estate through an overwhelming burden of encumbrances was unusual before the twentieth century.

3 Conclusion

What can be learnt from these settlement patterns? It is hard to generalise: every family pattern deserves investigation, for each illustrates some quirk, some eccentricity of the settlement which does not follow the model of the conveyancers' precedent books. Although the advice given to the family by the lawyers was obviously very important, the individual character of the settlor (particularly in a will, where he could conceal his arrangements from the family) was the most significant factor in deciding what the settlement should be.

How restrictive were settlements? A strict settlement, as long as it existed, restrained the life tenants in their dealings with the land. A very small number of entails included in settlements were inalienable, such as those granted by Parliament to Marlborough, Wellington, Abergavenny and Shrewsbury, but apart from these special cases, estates of families that practised settlement were periodically disentailed and resettled. At the time of disentailing the restrictions disappeared, although often similar ones were subsequently reimposed. Landed estates could, however, pass through the hands of several successive life tenants before the opportunity arose for disentailing, the opportunity being the existence, and agreement, of an adult tenant in tail.

It cannot be assumed that estates were disentailed and resettled every generation. As soon as the tenant in tail (usually unborn at the time of the settlement) came of age the settlement could be ended by disentailing; and in a straightforward case, where the settlement was made on marriage and an heir was born to the marriage who was named as tenant in tail, when that heir came of age the settlement could be broken. Three generations would have been involved; the bridegroom's father (the settlor), the bridegroom, and the heir: if the bridegroom's father had died before his son's wedding, then only two generations were involved.

But what if the bridegroom had no son? Then the settlement, if it was constructed in the usual way, would last all his life, and on his death the entail might take the estates to another male relative, pehaps a cousin who might already have had a son born when the original settlement was made. Then the cousin's grandson would be the tenant in tail (if one was eventually born) and the settlement would last through the settlor's life, his son's life, the cousin's life, the cousin's son's life, and finally be ended when the cousin's grandson came of age. In this way settlements could last a very long time. The entails established by strict settlement were not usually at an end if the direct line died out, for arrangements were normally included to involve more than one line. The settlement by will of Lowther of Whitehaven, proved in 1755, took Whitehaven to three different Lowther families before it was disentailed. The entails were usually dominated by male relations, and often the descent followed the rules of that of a peerage or baronetcy.

A man who succeeded as life tenant to the family lands was restricted by the family settlement; only a tenant in tail could inherit as a free agent. The family settlement histories outlined above only represent a small fraction of the hundreds of great landowning families that practised strict settlement, and so can only be used to offer impressions, not statistical certainties. The case histories suggest, however, that in each half century of the period of strict settlement, there were twice as many successions of life tenants as there were successions of tenants in tail. Several of the successions are difficult to categorise, such as that of an under-age daughter, or a tenant in tail whose estates were resettled by private act while he was still under age; but even if all the ambiguous cases were to be treated as successions of tenants in tail, their number would still be considerably less than those in the category of life tenant. The high mortality rates of the period around 1700, demonstrated by Hollingsworth in his studies of the demography of the British peerage and used by Bonfield in his work on family settlement, may have led to a rapid turnover in successions to estates, but the inclusion of complex entails and many collateral lines nevertheless produced a majority of successions of life tenants rather than tenants in tail: therefore a majority of men who at the time they inherited their family estates possessed only restricted powers over them.

The settlements that lasted longest were usually those made by will: an old man could name his son, grandson and possibly great-grandson, if one was already born, as successive life tenants, and the unborn great-great-grandson would then be tenant in tail, and the first person (on his majority) to be able to break the entail. The life tenants did not even have to be named: it was possible to put in a clause such as:

> Provided always, that if any person whom I have hereby made tenant in tail male of my said estates shall be born in my lifetime, then and in every such case I revoke the devise and appointment so made to him, and in lieu thereof I give, devise and appoint the hereditaments comprised in such devise and appointment, to the use of the same person respectively for the term of his natural life without impeachment of waste; and after his decease, to the use of his sons successively according to their respective seniorities in tail male . . . .[293]

In other words, a boy born while the settlor was dying would by this clause become another life tenant and not tenant in tail. Both the earls of Lonsdale and the Constables of Burton Constable used a similar clause in settlements.

A settlement made by will might last a hundred years. One small farm at North Frodingham, East Yorkshire, was strictly settled by will in 1726 and was still in settlement in 1814[294]. Thomas Coke's settlement of 1759 lasted 85 years[295]. The 1767 settlement of the Northumberland estates of the Percy dukes of Northumberland, lasted 39 years and a later settlement of 1817 on the same estates lasted 51 years[296]. Digby the 7th baron Middleton settled the bulk of his estates in 1848 on his cousin, his cousin's eldest son, his cousin's eldest grandson (all alive in 1848 and all life tenants), the son of the eldest grandson (he never married) and the second grandson and his son: it was a son of the second grandson who as the 11th baron Middleton was able to disentail in 1925, 77 years and four barons later[297]. Sir Clifford Constable's will, proved in 1870, settled the Burton Constable estates until his great-great-nephew came of age in 1912[298]. The Hotham settlement of 1787 lasted through the lifetime of four baronets and was only ended by the fifth, although this was not a settlement by will, but on the heir's coming of age (see above, pp.66–7).

Wills were of far greater importance in settlement patterns than have been recognised by twentieth-century historians. We may guess that every landowner made a will on inheriting, which settled his property at his death: to die intestate was virtually unknown among the landed classes. Often the provisional settlement in a young man's will would be overtaken by events, and altered as he married or as children were born: as obsolete wills were normally destroyed, it is only in rare cases that wills earlier in time than the last one are known.

Marriage settlements were of less importance in settling estates than settlements made on other occasions, a statement which is neutral in the important matter of the ways in which estates were enlarged. Often great families would settle only the jointure and portions on marriage (and sometimes these had already been limited by a previous settlement, made before the bride was known). In the patterns of family settlement cited here, there are about twice as many settlements by will as on marriage. A good deal more research into national and regional patterns is required before it can be affirmed that this is a general rule, but it is clear that to look at settlement in terms of marriage alone is quite unrealistic. It seems from the small sample of settlement patterns noted above that substantial settlements on marriage were more common around 1700 than they were later, but they never formed the majority; in the period 1660–1740 the categories of 'non-marriage' settlement and settlement by will each outnumbered those made on marriage (the figures are 9, 9 and 7). Over the whole period 1660–1880 the preponderance of 'non-marriage' settlements in the case histories over marriage settlements is much greater (approximately 37 to 13), although sometimes the nature of the settlement is ambiguous: for instance, into which category should a settlement be placed which was drawn up on the heir's coming of age subject to a general power which was subsequently revoked on marriage? Ambiguities apart, however, our sample is in any event too limited for us to attempt any national generalisations about the ratio of one type of settlement to another.

Most estates had unsettled lands that had either been deliberately left out of settlement or had been bought since the last settlement was made. It appears, without entering into controversial areas, that the unsettled lands were more often the result of the family's decision than demographic chance: the Cokes' settlements illustrate this well.

Private acts of Parliament were a common feature of settlement patterns. Most of the larger families investigated had at least one private act: the Cokes obtained six in 150 years. A private act was a more common expedient than a suit in Chancery, which was always unpopular: as Henry, viscount Lonsdale wrote in his will in 1747, he hoped his trustees would settle his affairs 'without having any suit Instituted in the Court of Chancery . . . to the end that the Persons to whom I desire to express my Friendship and Regard may not be deprived of the Benefit of it by the expensiveness and dilatoriness of that Court'[299].

Although it was possible for great estates to be broken up, the family histories given above make it clear that the land had to be unsettled (either through demographic accident or through deliberate and usually joint decision) before the estates could be dispersed. To this extent a strict settlement, as long as it lasted, protected the family's lands. By restricting the tenant for life to the income of the estates and preventing his access to the capital represented by the fee simple, settlement ensured that estates could and did survive spendthrifts, incompetents, and long minorities.

The same family histories demonstrate the extraordinary variety of settlement patterns. Although in principle the restraining influence of the strict settlement always tended to preserve the inheritance, in practice deeds framed by sophisticated conveyancers could be made to ensure or prevent almost anything that could happen to the estates. But once executed, the settlement could not be ended until the tenant in tail came of age: and until that day came, it took an act of Parliament to alter any detail of it.

Chapter III

Epilogue: The Historical Background. A Brief Survey

When a contributor to the *Edinburgh Review* wrote in April 1914 that:

> To anyone of middle age . . . the present public interest in the land must afford considerable matter for wonderment . . .

he was being false to the historical record. For over a century the land question in general and all matters relating to agriculture and rural affairs were never far from the more central concerns of domestic political discussion. There were many strands to this interest in land and rural society, and although their aims and objectives at times overlapped or coincided, the working-class and middle-class components must be clearly distinguished. It is with the middle-class critique and associated political agitation that this present brief discussion is concerned.

The early decades of the nineteenth century showed a remarkable complacency in the attitude of all propertied classes to the English land system. The classical economists and Benthamites were broadly in agreement concerning its efficiency; and despite Ricardo's strictures on the class of landlords there was general approval of the superiority of British agriculture and in particular of the large farm over the small holding. The Real Property Commissioners in 1829 emphasised what was an article of faith with those who controlled political power: that the law of real property in England, 'except in a few comparatively unimportant particulars, appears to come almost as near to perfection as can be expected in any human institutions'[300]. The seventh edition of the *Encyclopaedia Britannica* (1842) opened its 'General Observations on the Agriculture of Britain' with these words:

> The husbandry of a great part of Britain, both in respect to the cultivation of the soil and the breeding and management of live stock, is confessedly superior to that of any other country in Europe; and the

> quantity and value of its products, considering the character of the climate, as well as the industry, wealth and respectability of its husbandmen, are without any parallel either in ancient or modern times[301].

Agricultural productivity and the efficacy of the existing social structure in the countryside went together; and there were only a few areas in which critical argument was beginning. The cumbersome system of land transfer prompted a conveyancing barrister, James Humphreys, to bring out a small book in 1826 suggesting possible reforms. His comments provoked much discussion, and led, through Bentham's influence on Brougham, to a demand for legal changes[302]. The Real Property Commissioners, although they recorded their belief that the land law was 'near to perfection', did institute some land law reforms in the 1830s. There were other matters regarded as impediments to further progress: in the 1830s and 1840s there was already the beginnings of the debate about primogeniture and entail[303]; more technical agricultural questions included the important matter of restrictive covenants (there was a Select Committee in 1847–8) and compensation for unexhausted improvements. But what was not seriously questioned, except by ultra-radicals, were the basic principles upon which the British land system was based: the three-tiered structure of landlord, capitalist tenant farmer and landless labourer.

The context within which the arguments and discussions about land, and the laws governing land, took place, altered substantially during the third quarter of the nineteenth century. The repeal of the Corn Laws released middle-class radicals from the obsession of a decade, and they now appreciated more than ever the limited consequences of the first Reform Bill and Corn Law repeal in terms of political and social power. 'We have', Cobden wrote in 1849, 'the labour of Hercules in hand to abate the power of the aristocracy and their allies, the snobs of the towns.'[304] While Cobden and Bright could agree on the main political problems confronting radicals of their kind after 1846, they were not at one on matters of tactics and strategy. 'Our strength', Cobden wrote to Ashworth, 'lies with the shopocracy' but what did the shopocracy want? Not, Cobden emphasised, any large scheme of sudden organic change:

> The citadel of privilege in this country is so terribly strong, owing to the concentrated masses of property in the hands of comparatively few, that we cannot hope to assail it with success unless with the help of the propertied classes in the middle ranks of society, and by raising up a portion of the working-class to become members of a propertied order . . . [1 Oct. 1849]

Cobden had several policy suggestions to offer at this time, including the scheme for the forty-shilling freeholder, but on more fundamental political tactics such as the extension or partial extension of the franchise to those without property, there were wide disagreements between him and Bright; and it was these differences between them that accounted, in part, for the uncertainties and weaknesses of middle-class radicalism in the 1850s.

The movement for free trade in land, by which was meant the elimination of all legal restrictions upon the ownership and sale of real property, as a result of which land would become, like capital, a 'free' factor of production, got under way slowly. The problem had been referred to and discussed before 1850; the *Economist,* for example, from its earliest days, was arguing the case for the removal of restrictions upon the sale of land. What the *Economist* was concerned with was the application of *laissez-faire* principles to the ownership of land, and its management: a further extension of the mechanism of the market. The present settled estates, the argument went, were so encumbered with mortgages, debts and fixed payments to members of the family, that there was no money left for agricultural improvement and innovation. It was this concern with economic efficiency, and the ways in which settled estates hindered its full development, that remained central to the *Economist's* critique of the land laws; and the journal was arguing in the eighteen-seventies more or less what it had been saying in the fifties. The political consequences of free trade in land the *Economist* either denied or ignored. In 1855 the *Economist* developed its case:

> [At present] land cannot be obtained upon terms which induce men of capital and enterprise to embark in its cultivation with the same degree of energy as they enter into other industrial vocations of this country. And this obstacle is occasioned by the manner in which landed property is held and managed by its proprietors; for practically,

the occupiers of land are not the owners of it . . . .

So long as landed proprietors persist in retaining the nominal ownership of vast masses of land, which they have not the means to improve, and to the improvement of which by others their settlements offer an insuperable obstacle, neglected farms and slovenly cultivation will prevail as extensively as at present[305]

and two months later the *Economist* summed up 'the real source of the evil':

This is to be found in the system of settlements and entails by which men continue to regulate the ownership of land in the hands of a future generation[306].

The politics of the land question, especially in its 'free trade in land' aspect, were lifted to the level of a national debate by Cobden's last public speech in November 1864 at Rochdale. The most striking passage was to be much quoted:

If I were five-and-twenty or thirty, instead of being unhappily twice that number of years, I would take Adam Smith in hand – I would not go beyond him, I would have no politics in it – I would take Adam Smith in hand, and I would have a League for free trade in land just as we had a League for free trade in corn[307].

In spite of Cobden's disclaimer about politics, the Rochdale speech of this year and the previous year made a considerable impression upon public opinion; in 1863 there had been a public exchange of letters between Delane, the editor of *The Times*, and Cobden; and this was the beginning of what became a flood of articles, pamphlets and books. The 1861 Census had estimated the number of landed proprietors as 30,766 – a figure that was to be much bandied about by the landed reformers in the decade which followed – and although the 1871 Census tried to remedy matters by noting defensively 'that the number of small farmers is much greater than had generally been supposed, and that the English system of tenure and occupancy – however much it may admit of improvement in detail – is in principle admirably adapted to the circumstances of the people' – it was too late. When the earl of Derby in the House of Lords in 1872 referred to the 'clamour' against the landed monopoly in the country at large, he was not exaggerating. The results of the Return of Owners of Land, which Derby had persuaded the government to undertake, hardly supported his insistence that land was in fact widely distributed. The New Domesday Book, as the Return came to be popularly known, was both imperfect in the assembly and collection of data, and misleadingly presented[308]; but when the material had been analysed and rearranged – above all in the successive editions of John Bateman[309] – it was discovered that the degree of landed monopoly was more marked than most of the reformers had themselves claimed. G. C. Brodrick, summarising in 1881 what he thought was a sober estimate, found 'that a landed aristocracy consisting of about 2,250 persons own together nearly half the enclosed land in England and Wales', and he went on to note that estates in the other parts of the British Isles were on the average larger[310].

It was this landed monopoly, maintained and buttressed by the legal settlements which landed families practised in order to ensure the continuity of their estates through time, that the reformers were attacking. But the conclusions which were drawn by those who campaigned for 'free trade in land' differed widely. Although Cobden did not live to work out in detail the ideas of his Rochdale speech, Thorold Rogers, a close disciple, argued in *Cobden and Modern Political Opinion* (1873) that two consequences were expected: first, that a free market in land would benefit the farmers, because men with capital would then move into the farming sector, and encourage as high a rate of return on their investment as possible; and second, that the labouring class would be resettled on the land from which, in Cobden's phrase, they had been 'divorced'. In other words, the removal of all legal hindrances to the easy and economical transfer of land would encourage the revival of peasant proprietorship. It was an extraordinary business, this concern with a peasantry in the most urban and most proletarianised society in the world. Before 1840 there had been scant support for the small man and the small property; middle- and upper-class opinion fairly unanimously accepted the ideas of popularisers such as J. R. McCulloch who strongly opposed the subdivision of holdings on the grounds of the supposed inefficiency of peasant agriculture; and to this condemnation of the wastefulness of petty proprietorship was linked a Malthusian assumption which correlated a tendency towards increasing subdivision of land with a greater than average population growth. France, and especially Ireland, were the sources for most arguments of these kinds, and it was mainly the later travellers' reports from Western Europe, and J. S. Mill's own close study of the Irish situation, that produced during the 1840's a vigorous reaction against these received ideas. Mill's conversion to an advocacy of peasant proprietorship has been much discussed[311] and within twenty years of the first edition of the *Principles* in 1848 his ideas on this question were the common stock of many working-class as well as some middle-class radicals. In the Land Tenure Reform Association, Mill, before his death in 1873, had a political organisation through which his ideas on the land question could be publicised. Most middle-class opinion which was in support of the demands for free trade in land did not, however, argue or expect any substantial or even partial transformation of the economic and social structure of the countryside. The mainstream of liberal opinion, such as William Fowler[312] or the *Economist*, were quite certain that market forces would operate in the land market as in other sectors of the economy; as the *Economist* put it in 1870, a free market in land 'could only attract those with capital'; and these would certainly not include the contemporary labouring classes.

The agitation for free trade in land diminished appreciably in the 1880s, and even in its mid-Victorian form it was never a political movement of any consequence. It is worth inquiring, briefly, why this was so, for it is indeed one of the minor paradoxes of nineteenth-century politics that an agitation which aroused so much interest had so little effect in practical terms. A. V. Dicey, in an article in the *Law Quarterly Review* in 1905, addressed himself to this question, and his answers offer a beginning to a more general analysis: although Dicey, it must be noted, did not separate out at all clearly the different strands to the anti-landed monopoly agitation. Dicey began by insisting that the 'incessant modifications or reforms of the law, which extend over seventy years . . . have left unchanged, in a sense almost untouched, the fundamentals of the law with regard to land.' He suggested three reasons: first, the complexity of the law of real estate, the technical difficulties of amendment and the powerful vested interests of the conveyancers; secondly, that land law reform never became a politically effective demand of major importance; and third, that in the previous quarter of a century, there had occurred a growing division of opinion between radicals of the mid-Victorian kind and the young socialists of the 1880s[313]. Bradlaugh, not mentioned by Dicey, illustrated very well the hostility of a radical of the 'old-fashioned' sort to the socialist movement of his last decade[314]. There were, of course, other reasons not referred to by Dicey; the most important being the economic depression in agriculture which altered the general context within which landowners operated. While the impact of depression was very different in different parts of the country, the depreciation of farming profits, the abatement and absolute decrease in rents, the diminished capital value of agricultural land, all contributed to changes of magnitude in the long-term situation of the landowning classes. The crucial decade was probably the 1880s and as Cannadine has commented the new factors of 'declining revenue and eroded confidence'[315] meant that the landed orders were increasingly on the defensive. Encumbrances and debts of all kinds now became much harder to service, and this was an essential part of the background of the marked activity in the land market during the second half of the 1890s and the early years of the twentieth century and also in the immediate aftermath of the First World War[316]. But there were also straight political reasons why the land question after 1880 was no longer discussed in mid-Victorian terms. Preoccupation with Ireland and the Irish question hardened attitudes among the ruling groups against land reform in other parts of Britain, at the same time as there were also new ideas about land which shifted the arguments to more radical considerations. The impact of Henry George and the idea of the single tax was markedly influential upon Liberal thinking, and the land question remained part of the politics of the radical wing of the Party until the First World War[317]. For the young socialist movement of the 1880s, however, land was no longer any more important than other factors of production; indeed, in an overwhelmingly urban, industrialised society it was less significant, and henceforth land was joined to those other means of production which required to be taken into public ownership if capitalism was to be superseded.

The continuing interest in the land question in general, and the concern with the peculiarities of land tenure in Britain compared with the rest of Europe, encouraged a growing study of the history of the English landed system. In the three or four decades before 1914 there took place a remarkable outpouring of learned writing on the origins and subsequent history of land tenures and rural social structures. Leaving aside the great legal historians who were especially interested in mediaeval society, the ways in which the eighteenth-century rural structure came into being – differentiating it so sharply from any other in Europe – attracted a long list of scholars of whom Tawney and the Hammonds are the best known; but among others there were Slater, Hasbach, Levy, Johnson, Gonner and Ernle. By contrast, the years between the wars saw relatively little historical research and certainly a marked decline in general interest: not at all surprising given the urban problems of these years. The land question was no longer what it was in 1900: the position of the tenant farmers had begun to alter in that increasing numbers were now owners of the farms they cultivated; many large estates began to be broken up; and the 1925 Law of Property Act was the final stage in the legal dismantling of the type of strict settlement against which the agitation of the mid-Victorian reformers had been directed. When serious historical discussion began again, with the publication of John Habakkuk's first article at the end of the inter-war period, the context had quite altered, and the assumptions underlying the analysis and debate which followed in the post-war years, were now almost wholly academic.

The new stage of academic scholarship began with Habakkuk's seminal article of 1940. Summarising his work on estates in Northamptonshire and Bedfordshire he noted that:

> The general drift of property in the sixty years after 1690 was in favour of the large estate and the great lord; and while the movement was probably not so decisive as that which, in the hundred years before 1640 consolidated the squirearchy, it clearly marks one of the great changes in the disposition of English landed property[318].

In the four decades which have followed the publication of his first article Habakkuk enlarged and extended, and at times somewhat amended, the original thesis of 1940. His main arguments can be summarised thus: first, that between the late seventeenth century and the middle of the eighteenth century the numbers of great landowners, and their acreage, increased notably, and as one consequence the market in agricultural land became a good deal more restricted by the end of the eighteenth century. Second, the stricter forms of settlement which developed during the second half of the seventeenth century, assisted by a parallel improvement in long-term mortgages, impeded the alienation of his property by the life tenant, and thereby favoured the preservation of great estates. Third, the stricter forms of settlement also promoted the accumulation of estates through marriage with heiresses with land, or brides who brought large portions into the marriage: money that was usually spent on buying land.

Over the years Habakkuk offered certain qualifications and changes of emphasis to his original analysis; and other historians have contributed other, sometimes more substantial criticisms; but often, as with so much agrarian research, inevitably limited to particular counties or regions. On a national plane, F. M. L. Thompson, in three articles, argued that the distribution of land between estates of different sizes remained remarkably stable, and altered only slowly between 1641 and 1873[319]; and in a late article (1979) Habakkuk accepted that there could be doubt on this matter of size distribution over time. If Thompson's argument continues to be accepted, and is buttressed in the future by further analysis of admittedly difficult statistical data, then it will alter certain of Habakkuk's assumptions about the role of strict settlement in the historical process of the growth of the large estate. But it will shift the emphasis of his arguments, and not destroy them. If it is to be accepted that from the late seventeenth century the proportion of land owned by the great landlords, and the gentry, was always considerable, then in an economy in which the tempo of economic change was quickening, the emergence of stricter settlements undoubtedly promoted the *preservation* of estates and offset the centrifugal tendencies of a developing market economy. There are, of course, a whole range of questions that require further research, including the crucial question of the disappearance of the peasantry, and its timing: a matter considered in the important article by Habakkuk in *Annales* in 1965[320]. But what has to be appreciated once again is the variety of settlement experience, and the ingenuity of conveyancers and solicitors in elaborating new legal techniques for achieving stability in spite of generational hazards. No doubt, in addition to the improved availability of mortgages in the eighteenth century, there were other sources of credit that worked in the same direction, as Thompson has reminded us,[321] but the examples which have been set out in the previous chapters of this monograph have made it clear that in spite of the undoubted tendencies to dispersal that threatened all large and middling estates, the legal developments associated with the many forms of the strict settlement encouraged and fostered their cohesion through time. Stricter and more elaborate forms of entail, and the provision for quite remote contingencies, kept family estates within the kinship group; and Habakkuk's general thesis has certainly been vindicated in terms of the preservation argument.

In the matter of marriages and their consequences the analysis is by no means agreed. Clay and Beckett have offered criticisms[322], and a good deal more research will be needed before the matter can be definitively pronounced upon; and the same is true of the characteristics of the land market at different periods within the two hundred years to 1900. But there is one important question derived from Habakkuk that must be firmly revised. In his 1953 article, referring to strict settlement, Habakkuk wrote that 'these arrangements were most commonly made at the marriage of the heir'[323] and in 1979 he omitted the qualification, stating firmly that succession to estates was 'laid down in a family settlement, made at his [the owner's] marriage or his father's marriage'[324]. The assumption has mostly been accepted and one historian, Bonfield, based a whole article on the hypothesis that strict settlement was equivalent to marriage settlement[325]. Once this fallacy is understood, and the variety of settlement practices accepted, the preservation thesis is greatly strengthened. Whatever the nature or the timing of individual family settlements, most could and would last through quite dramatic demographic casualties in any one family or kinship group. As has been shown above, settlements made by will usually lasted for much longer than settlements made at marriage: on occasion for almost a century. The variety of types of settlements available and the flexibility of legal devices at the command of conveyancers, and settlors of estates, all made their individual and collective contribution to the high proportion of land owned by the aristocracy and gentry which lasted through to the end of the nineteenth century: a remarkable and unique phenomenon of British society.

As for the arguments of the Victorian land reformers concerning the economic consequences of settled estates upon the desired levels of capital investment and the efficiency of farm management, any definitive conclusions still elude us until more work has been done on a national basis. Caird in 1878 was in no doubt that landowners have spent 'a much larger sum . . . from their own resources' than had come from either the State or the Drainage and Improvement companies[326]; but a statement of this kind, whatever its validity, is no answer to the central question. Mid-Victorian borrowing by the aristocracy was certainly on a considerable scale; but in the prosperous years to 1880, the size of debt was not an adequate basis upon which any argument can be based about the efficiency or otherwise of the settled estate as an economic unit '. . . debt, but not ruinous debt', Cannadine has noted, 'was a common feature of life for many landed families'; and it was only the fall in farming profitability, and rents, that made the servicing of debt a serious problem[327]. For these mid-Victorian years we require more case studies; and until these are forthcoming, the argument sometimes adduced, and certainly arguable, that the land reformers were mostly basing their attacks upon economic myths of their own making, will not be resolved[328]. By contrast, the political consequences of strict settlement – the support and preservation of the political and social power of the landed aristocracy and gentry – were, of course, substantial.

List of Abbreviations used in the Notes

Further details of the works are given in the bibliography and list of short titles, pp.132–7. Acts of Parliament are cited in the form 2 Geo.III c.6. For the method of citing reports of law cases, see pp.123–4, note 131.

Amer. J. of Legal Hist.	*American Journal of Legal History*
Annales ESC	*Annales, économies, sociétés, civilisations*
C. & W.A. & A.S.	*Cumberland & Westmorland Antiquarian & Archaeological Society*
Cal. S.P. Dom.	*Calendar of State Papers, Domestic*
Camb. Law J.	*Cambridge Law Journal*
CRO	County Record Office
Cumbria CRO, D/Lons	Cumbria County Record Office, Lonsdale archives
DNB	*Dictionary of National Biography*
Econ. Hist. Rev.	*Economic History Review*
H. of Lords MSS	*House of Lords Manuscripts*
HCCRO DDBR	Humberside County Record Office, Bower archives
HCCRO DDCC	Humberside County Record Office, Chichester Constable archives
HCCRO DDCL	Humberside County Record Office, Clark archives
HCCRO DDSA	Humberside County Record Office, Saltmarshe archives
HCCRO DDSD	Humberside County Record Office, Scholfield archives
HCCRO DDX	Humberside County Record Office, miscellaneous archives
HFD	Holkham Family Deeds
HMC	*Historical Manuscripts Commission*, reports
HUL DDHO	Hull University Library, Hotham archives
HUL DDSY	Hull University Library, Sykes archives
Huntington Lib. Q.	*Huntington Library Quarterly*
NUL Mi	Nottingham University Library, Middleton archives
NUL Ne	Nottingham University Library, Newcastle archives
NRA	National Register of Archives
NYCRO ZDS	North Yorkshire County Record Office, Downe archives
NYCRO ZFY	North Yorkshire County Record Office, Bower archives
OED	*Oxford English Dictionary*
PP	Parliamentary Papers
PRO	Public Record Office
TRHS	*Transactions of the Royal Historical Society*
VCH	Victoria County History of England

Notes

Notes 1–12 for pages 11–15 (for abbreviations and short titles see pp.116, 132–40)

Note. The counties referred to in this work are the historic counties, as they existed until the year 1973.

1. Irish settlements were very similar to those made in England, but in Scotland the land law was very different; from 1685 it was possible to create a form of perpetual entail, and it was not until the Rutherford Act of 1848 that Scots entails could be barred. Settlements of land in Wales were the same as those in England; Farran 1958; Wylie 1975. A Scottish entail, of the estates of the earldom of Mar, made in 1740, is printed in full (except for the enumeration of lands) in Cokayne 1910–59, IX (1936) 121–34.
2. Statutory definitions of settlement have been given at various times, notably in the Settled Land Acts of 1882 and 1925. See discussion in Harvey 1973, 19–20.
3. Bridgeman's precedents were published by his clerk after his death, and went through many editions from 1682. Davidson's precedents similarly went through many editions from 1844. See Bridgeman 1682 and Davidson 1844–85 in the bibliography (below, pp.132, 133).
4. Burke 1869.
5. HCCRO DDSA/641; Thompson 1963, 66.
6. The two main types are the strict settlement, and the trust for sale, or so-called trader's settlement, because it was most commonly used by merchants or men who owned a mixture of interests that could not be dealt with as freehold. Trusts for sale were not commonly used by landowners. See Lightwood 1929.
7. The term strict settlement seems to have first been used in 1710; *OED* IX (1919) 1120.
8. It was possible until the Statute of Frauds (1677) to transfer land without any kind of document, the transfer being marked by some physical act. But documentary proof became more and more necessary, and after 1677 was required by law. The types of documents used in making settlements are shown in the table below, which includes the dates at which they were introduced, were abolished, or became obsolete (represented by . . . .)

Type of document	*Introduced*	*Abolished/obsolete*
Will	Anglo-Saxon era or earlier	Still current
Feoffment with livery of seisin	11th cent. or earlier	1845 . . . .
Fine	12th cent.	1833
Common recovery	c.1472	1833
Bargain and sale	16th cent.	late 17th cent.
Lease and release	c.1615	1841 . . . .
Disentailing assurance	1833	Still current
Release alone	1841	1845
Deed of grant	1845	1925

9. Pollock 1883, 113.
10. See Glossary, pp.138–40.
11. Four out of the five Northamptonshire families studied by Dr Finch were using this method by the early seventeenth century: Finch 1956, 167. In a much larger number of families, Dr Bonfield found 'life estate-entail settlement' was the prevailing form in Kent and Northamptonshire in the first half of the seventeenth century; Bonfield 1978, 130.
12. For pre-1640 examples of these settlements, see Williams 1858, 45–9; Pollock 1883,

Notes 13–18 for pages 15–17 (for abbreviations and short titles see pp.116, 132–40)

app.G; Finch 1956, many examples, e.g. 23, 51, 56, 78–9, 98, 103, 125–6, 143–4, 152–3; Cooper 1976, 204 and n.

13. The attribution of the device of the trustees to preserve contingent remainders to Bridgeman was recorded c.1750; Blackstone 1765–9, II 172. See Williams 1858; Pollock 1883, app.G; Holdsworth 1922–57 VII (1925) 112 and nn. Orlando Bridgeman, 1606?–1674, was called to the bar 1632, chief justice of Chester 1638, attorney of the Court of Wards and solicitor general to the Prince of Wales in 1640. He was in Parliament in 1640 and knighted in 1643. As a royalist, after the death of the king he gave up the bar and practised privately as a conveyancer, being forbidden to live in London. He was given office on the Restoration; became Lord Keeper in 1667 and resigned in 1672. His contemporary Geoffrey Palmer, 1598–1670, was called to the bar in 1623. As a royalist he held no office until 1660, when he was made attorney general, which he remained until his death. Palmer was a very learned lawyer, but according to Roger North, whose brother Francis owed his rapid advancement to Palmer, he never wrote down his 'collections' but kept his legal knowledge in his head (North 1826, I 23). Bridgeman's model conveyances were printed after his death by his clerk, and it is possibly because Bridgeman's precedents were published and Palmer's were not recorded that Bridgeman obtained the major share of the credit for using trustees to preserve contingent remainders. He was called the 'Father of modern conveyancing', Holdsworth 1922–57, VII (1925) 377.

    Part of the preface to the 1689 edition of Bridgeman's *Conveyances* reads:

    > These Precedents need no other Encomium, than that they were the Draughts of that Eminent and Learned Person, the late Lord Keeper Bridgeman; framed and advised by him during the time of his Pactice [*sic*]; when the unhappy Circumstances wherein this Kingdom stood, afforded no other means of Safety to Persons of his Loyalty and Constancy, than a strict Retirement from all Publick Affairs . . . betaking himself to a Sedentary kind of Life in his Chamber, he became the great Oracle, not only of his Fellow Sufferers, but of the whole Nation in Matters of Law; his very Enemies not thinking their Estates secure without his Advice . . . . Then it was, That these Precedents were framed and advised by him; they being for the most part Settlements between Persons of the greatest Honour in the Kingdom.

    Dr Bonfield has collected evidence to show that Bridgeman did not in fact use trustees to preserve contingent remainders in his own family settlements in 1648 or 1658, but did so in 1670. Palmer, on the other hand, did include the trustees in his son's successive settlements of 1654, 1664 and 1667; Bonfield 1978, 138, 148–50.
14. Bridgeman 1689, 128. The date is from the description of R. earl of Essex as 'Lord Chamberlain', which was only true of 1641–2.
15. North 1826, I 146–8; date of the will from Cokayne 1910–59, IX (1936) 657. North had been Palmer's clerk.
16. *OED* IX (1919) 1120. The classic work on contingent remainders is Fearne 1772 (and later editions). The law relating to contingent remainders was altered in 1845 and again in 1877; after 1877 trustees to preserve the contingent remainders became unnecessary: Underhill 1901.
17. The rule was finally established that any interest in property must vest (that is, take effect) within a life or lives in being at the date of the instrument (or, if by will, at the settlor's death) plus 21 years plus a period of gestation.
18. A clear exposition of what the life tenant's powers would be under the 1882 act is given

Notes 19–35 for pages 16–24 (for abbreviations and short titles see pp.116, 132–40)

(prospectively) by N. T. Lawrence, in his evidence to the Richmond Commission; PP 1881, 834–41.

19. Sugden 1861, ix–xxii.
20. See below, pp.49–52.
21. For example, Vanbrugh's plays, George Eliot's *Felix Holt,* Jane Austen's *Pride and Prejudice,* passages from Greville's diaries and Horace Walpole's papers, and Hogarth's 'Marriage à la Mode'.
22. Listed in Maxwell and Maxwell (1955). MS volumes of precedents can be found in many county record offices. For instance, a Colchester firm of solicitors kept books of copies of deeds and wills from 1704–1803 (Essex CRO); Messrs Stenton & Metcalfe, Southwell solicitors, used a book of precedents written at intervals between the late seventeenth century and early nineteenth century, which was a mixture of conveyances the solicitors had drawn, extracts from Blackstone's *Commentaries,* and precedents copied from Horsman's *Precedents in Conveyancing* (Notts CRO DDM/159/4); another MS precedent book in the same CRO (1654–1752, 2 vols) is M/356–7. Norfolk CRO has many volumes of precedents (Aylsham MS 4385, T 188C; MS 4386, T 138C), and Hertfordshire CRO has precedent books of the seventeenth to nineteenth centuries (D/EHa B13–26; D/EL B499).
23. Park 1833, 19–20.
24. Humphreys 1826, 164.
25. Williams 1862, 597. Compare with the comment of E. B. Denison (later Lord Grimthorpe) to a younger lawyer, and relation, about his own settlement in 1870: 'I have only taken the liberty (which made my drafts very unpopular with solicitors) of erasing a good deal of the usual rubbish. I don't advise you to do it with a view to your own success, but when you are "killing your own mutton" there is no need of superfluous flourishes of the knife'; HCCRO DDSD/49w.
26. Warwickshire CRO CR 114A/8.
27. Crust Todd Mills & Co solicitors, Beverley; HUL, DDSY.
28. 'Commentary on Mr Humphreys' Real Property Code', Bowring 1843, 392, repr. from *Westminster Review* VI (Oct. 1826).
29. Williams 1862, 601.
30. Bythewood and Jarman 1821–36, X (1834) 418–36. For example, under the eighteenth-century will of Sir George Savile, anyone named in the Savile settlement who became earl of Scarbrough could not keep the Savile property too, but must pass it on to the next in succession; Beastall 1975, 10. A similar clause to the shifting use was the springing use, a use which 'sprang' into effect after the settlement was made. See Williams 1879, 23–4.
31. After 1833 he was called the 'protector' of the settlement.
32. Spring, E. 1964, 214.
33. Spring, E. 1964, 213n; evidence given by N. T. Lawrence, PP 1881, 834–41. To cite examples of the heir's annuity, at the Sykes family settlement of 1792, the heir received an annuity of £500 in his father's lifetime, which he gave up on marriage for a settlement of some of the family's lands (HUL, DDSY/108/13, 20); in 1847 another Sykes heir received during his father's lifetime an annuity of £1500 as a bachelor and £4000 after marriage; and finally in 1900 a third Sykes heir received during his father's lifetime £2000 a year, increasing to £3000 in 1904 and £5000 in 1909 (Crust Todd Mills & Co solicitors, Beverley).
34. Bythewood and Jarman 1821–36, IX (1833) 212–43.
35. Lewis 1937–81, 36 (1973) 297. Because of the doctrine that a conveyance of land must be

Notes 36–51 for pages 24–7 (for abbreviations and short titles see pp.116, 132–40)

made in return for 'good consideration' it was difficult to settle property on a servant or on a friend who was not related to the settlor.

36. Thompson 1965, 23–44.
37. 2 Anne c.6 (Ir.).
38. Trumbach 1978, 74.
39. There is an extensive literature on primogeniture. See, for instance, Kenny 1878; Brodrick 1881; Maitland 1911; Thirsk 1969. Rubinstein 1981, 134 has shown that primogeniture was not typical of *non*-landed wealth-holders in the second half of the nineteenth century, who favoured equal division. In our case histories both a Hotham and a Lowther were disinherited; see pp.63–4, 74.
40. Boswell 1970, 548.
41. Holdsworth 1922–57, VII (1925) 149–50. Standard works on powers are Powell 1787, Sugden 1808 and Farwell 1874.
42. Pin-money is first recorded in 1542, for a daughter; 'I give my said daughter Margaret my lease of the parsonage of Kirkdale . . . to buy her pins.' Other seventeenth-century instances of the word refer to an allowance to a mistress. Vanbrugh uses the phrase pin-money in a play published in 1697. In 1712 Addison referred to it as a recent innovation (all references from *OED* VII 887).
43. Sugden 1858, 141; Williams 1879, 129.
44. Bythewood and Jarman 1821–36, IX (1833) 213, 215. See also Stone 1965, 635. Some men objected to the independence pin-money gave their wives; Trumbach 1978, 81 n.46, 83.
45. Trumbach collected 62 examples of the jointure/portion ratio for peers from the eighteenth century and found 10 per cent the usual proportion; Trumbach 1978, 82. Other examples are given by Habakkuk 1950, 25; Stone 1965, 645; Roebuck 1980, 88, 173; Thompson 1963, 100–3. On the Sledmere estates under a settlement of 1801 the jointure of the life tenant's widow was to be not more than £80 per £1000 of the wife's portion, with a top limit of £1500 if one jointress, and £1500 and £1000 if two (HUL DDSY/110/30). Two younger brothers, having smaller estates settled on them, were limited to £500 p.a. and £400 p.a. without regard to their wives' dowries. In 1847, on the same Sledmere estates, the life tenant was allowed to raise a jointure of £4000 for one widow, and £6000 in total if more than one, again without regard to the dowry (settlements at Crust Todd Mills & Co solicitors, Beverley). On the Burton Constable estates under the settlement of 1791, life tenants were able to charge the estates with not more than £500 with a total limit of £2500 p.a. (envisaging five widows!) without regard to dowry. In 1827 and again in 1870, £1000 in jointure was permitted on the Burton Constable estate (HCCRO DDCC). Of course no Englishman could have more than one widow; but these arrangements envisaged a succession of life tenants leaving widows as dependents of the estates.
46. Sugden 1858, 137.
47. Dower estates can be identified in, for instance, Bateman 1883, 30, 137, 331.
48. Cooper 1976, 212, 228; Trumbach 1978, 88–9. On portions see Williams 1879, 259–87.
49. Roger North's sisters' portions were to be provided for by sale: 'His lordship's father designed some skirts of his estate to be sold, to raise 1500 L a-piece for their portions', North 1826, II 225.
50. Trumbach 1978, 60.
51. Stone 1965, 633n; Williams 1879, 280–1.

Notes 52–76 for pages 27–32 (for abbreviations and short titles see pp.116, 132–40)

52. Habakkuk 1950; Mingay 1963: Stone 1965: Roebuck 1980.
53. Holdsworth 1922–57, VII (1925) 175. It was not until Lord Hardwicke's Marriage Act of 1753 that the marriage of persons under 21 without their father's or guardian's consent was illegal. Until 1753, therefore, the runaway child, whose portion was settled, was a valuable property.
54. Elphinstone 1900, 348.
55. The Settled Estates Acts of 1856 and 1877 altered this position, but they were both permissive acts and could be excluded from a settlement.
56. Sugden 1858, 129, 151; Williams 1879, 309. In Trumbach's study of thirty eighteenth-century families, he found only two great estates where the life tenant took fines: Trumbach 1978, 74 and n.8.
57. Elphinstone 1900, 232.
58. The power to grant building leases was so commonly included in the nineteenth century, that 'when the marquis of Stafford's solicitors saw the date 1833 on a settlement, they did not trouble to read it, but acted on the assumption that it contained powers to grant building leases': wrongly, as it turned out. Spring, E. 1977, 45.
59. For waste see Sugden 1858, 151–3; Williams 1879, 228–39; Riddall 1979, 57–60.
60. On copyholds and leaseholds see Sugden 1858, 84; Elphinstone 1900, 396–7.
61. Williams 1879, 320; evidence of N. T. Lawrence to the Richmond Commission, PP 1881, 834–41. The legislation of the nineteenth century under which tenants for life could borrow for agricultural improvements was discussed in Spring, D. 1963, 136–61. See also Underhill 1901, 282; Dicey 1905; Spring, E. 1964; Spring, E. 1977.
62. Holdsworth 1922–57, VII (1925) 169–70.
63. The power of revocation was considered by Heneage Finch for inclusion in his son's settlement of the 1670s; Bonfield 1981, 109 from *HMC Finch MSS* II (1922) 17–18.
64. Hayes and Jarman 1863, 6ln; Williams 1879, 40–1.
65. Pollock 1896, 118.
66. Underhill 1901, 282.
67. Thompson 1963, 65–8.
68. The eleven families who held more than 10,000 acres in the 1870s were (in alphabetical order) Bethell, Broadley, Cholmley, Constable, Downe, Hotham, Leconfield, Londesborough, Middleton, Sykes and Wenlock; PP 1875.
69. The only one of the eleven families that did not practise strict settlement was the Broadley family. Examples of intervals between settlements can be found in the case histories below; see, for example, pp.65–6, 79.
70. Gover 1889, 49.
71. Williams 1879, 352–3; Underhill 1901, 300.
72. Barlow 1957, 197.
73. Coke 1832, 187.
74. Barlow 1957, 197–226; Kenny 1879, 104.
75. Clifford 1885–7, I 403, 410.
76. Only by an express act of the parties did the property become separate estate; the great change of the Married Women's Property Act of 1870 was that certain categories of women's property (e.g. their earnings, and property acquired by women married after the Act) became separate at once. See Kenny 1879, 113–14. The wife's separate estate was sometimes seen by the husband as a threat to his authority; the bride of Sir Dudley North burnt her separate settlement before she went (c.1682) to church to be married (an

Notes 70–109 for pages 32–41 (for abbreviations and short titles see pp.116, 132–40)

act of destruction which Roger North thought very proper). North 1826, III 118–20. The alterations in women's position as property owners are shown in Trumbach 1978, 81–3.

77. See above, p.12.
78. Bridgeman 1725, 369.
79. Roebuck 1980, 220–1, 229—30.
80. There is a long and interesting account of this transaction in Lewis 1937–81, 36 (1973) 24–32 and 'Case of the entail', app.1, 295–304. The arrangement was overturned by a later codicil added by the 3rd earl.
81. HCCRO DDCC/144/24, correspondence of May 1827.
82. HUL DDSY(2)/1/2a. See also Adelson 1975, 72–4.
83. The mean and median age at marriage of peers' children is given by Hollingsworth 1964, 11, 25 and tables 2, 27; discussed also by Bonfield 1979, 483–92.
84. Spring, E. 1964, 214–15.
85. Trumbach 1978, 75.
86. Bythewood and Jarman 1821–36, IX (1833) 29–56.
87. NUL Mi F 7.
88. *H. of Lords MSS* NS XII (1977) 373. The records of the House of Lords contain many other examples of settlements made on behalf of minors by means of private estate acts.
89. For instance, Lord Warrington in 1701 arranged for his uncle, George Booth, to negotiate marriage between him and one of the two daughters of a rich London merchant. The marriage brokers Isaackson and Towers were to have 1000 guineas to make the match: *H. of Lords MSS* NS X (1953) no.3071. There was no legislation against marriage brokers, but ultimately the courts would not enforce any payments due to them, which made their position impossible; Trumbach 1978, 100–2.
90. For a discussion of marriage motives in seventeenth-century England, see Slater 1976; Mendelson and Slater 1979; also Trumbach 1978.
91. Blundell 1952, 5–6.
92. Margerison 1886, 113–15. The spelling of the quotation has been modernised.
93. Elphinstone 1900, 431.
94. Sir John Reresby's Memoirs, quoted by Turberville 1938–9, I (1938) 225n.
95. Tyrer and Bagley 1972, xi.
96. Lewis 1937–81, 36 (1973) 296.
97. *Huguenin* v. *Baseley* (1807) 14 Ves. Jun. 273; White and Tudor 1910, I 295–302.
98. Spring, E. 1964, 221. For other examples of settlements made by will, see Trumbach 1978, 49.
99. PP 1833, 3 and n.
100. Crane 1957, 227.
101. Turberville 1938–9, I (1938) 302–27; Davies 1965, 45–6; Kelch 1974, 28.
102. Burke 1869, I 195.
103. Margerison 1886, 65n.
104. Blundell 1952, 148; Tyrer and Bagley 1970, 49–50.
105. HCCRO DDCC/130/246, 248.
106. Margerison 1886, 143–4.
107. Smith 1928, 186, 190.
108. HUL DDSY/98/78.
109. Ellis 1974, 133–5.

Notes 110–31 for pages 42–6 (for abbreviations and short titles see pp.116, 132–40)

110. Lewis 1937–81, 36 (1973) app.1, 295–304.
111. *Snell* v. *Silock* (1800) 5 Ves. Jun. 474.
112. Phillips 1979, 210.
113. *Sir John Trevor's estate* 1 Eq. Ca. Abr. 388.
114. Spring, E. 1977, 45.
115. Spring, D. 1963, 128.
116. *Garth* v. *Sir John Hind Cotton* (1750) 1 Ves. Sen. 524, 546.
117. Kerly 1890, 199.
118. Although some trustees were alleged to make money from their trust. The sole surviving trustee of the first earl of Leicester, Ralph Cauldwell, was alleged to have made nearly £40,000 in a few years (Parker 1975, 66) and similar accusations were made against the descendant of the sole surviving trustee of the early nineteenth-century Constable estates in East Yorkshire, Robert Dyneley (HCCRO DDCC/133/24).
119. Bridgeman 1689, 128–35.
120. Parker 1975, 1; HCCRO DDCC/134/61. The solicitor was Dyneley, who also acted for the Yorkshire Downe family, and the Sykes of Sledmere. The firm of Dyneley and Ashmall, of Gray's Inn, had, according to an inquiry made in 1780, defended more than 20 prosecutions of Catholic families under the penal laws, and had defended them without charge. Robson 1959, 76n.
121. HCCRO DDCC/133/24.
122. Thompson 1958, 122.
123. HUL DDSY and HCCRO DDX/31.
124. *Mansell* v. *Mansell* (1732) 2 P Wms 681; *Vernon* v. *Vaudrey* (1740) Barn. 303.
125. This and the preceding paragraphs are based on Lewin 1928, 937–63.
126. Park 1833, p.iv. On the social history of the legal profession, see Carr-Saunders and Wilson 1933; Robson 1959; Birks 1960; Harding 1966; Abel-Smith and Stevens 1967.
127. Spring and Spring 1956, 172.
128. HCCRO DDCC.
129. Unfortunately it seems to be impossible to find the papers of a complete London conveyancing practice. The ravages of time, dispersal of archives, bombing (especially of London) during the Second World War, and the policy of the British Records Association, which has been to divide lawyers' papers between county record offices according to the families involved, have all contributed to the regrettable absence of complete sets of conveyancing archives. The British Records Association's practice is of course understandable but it does mean that it is not possible to see the work of a firm as a whole. This comment is based on inquiries to the National Register of Archives, all county record offices and the major archive repositories in addition to the counties.
130. HUL DDSY.
131. The main sources of Chancery cases are the different series of law reports: *The English Reports* from the sixteenth century to 1865 (165 volumes of all kinds, reprinted from private, unofficial reports); from 1865 on, the official *Law Reports*. Other reports were published in the *Law Journal Reports* and the *Law Times Reports*. Normally pre-1865 cases are cited in the form *Jarndyce* v. *Jarndyce* (1820) 2 Ves. Jun. 680, representing the parties, the date of the hearing, the volume number and the name of the reporter, and the page number in the original report. Post 1865 cases are cited as *Jarndyce* v. *Jarndyce* [1870] 2 K.B. 831, indicating the parties, the date of the report, the volume of that year, the abbreviation for the official court report (in this case King's Bench) and the page

Notes 132–57 for pages 46–51 (for abbreviations and short titles see pp.116, 132–40)

number. Hearing dates are in round brackets: report dates in square.

132. White and Tudor 1910, I 265. It was the practice to employ separate legal advisers for heirs who were joining their parents or relatives in a resettlement, to rule out allegations of undue influence.
133. White and Tudor 1910, I 259–302, from *Huguenin* v. *Baseley* (1807) 14 Ves. Jun. 273.
134. Squibb 1959.
135. Kerly 1890, 218–20; White and Tudor 1910, I 578–603.
136. HCCRO DDCC/134/79.
137. Cokayne 1910–59, II (1912) 315–16n.
138. See, for instance, the legal opinions sought by the Russells after the execution of Lord William Russell in 1683: Thomson 1937, 388–9.
139. There is a list in Cokayne 1910–59, I (1910) app.E. The names on the list are mostly Scots.
140. Cokayne 1910–59, IV (1916) 225.
141. *H. of Lords MSS* NS XII (1977) xxxii, 437.
142. Roebuck 1980, 157–8; Aveling 1960.
143. HCCRO DDSY/98/78 and 108/25.
144. For one of the many indictments of Chancery proceedings from the late seventeenth century to the nineteenth century, see Kerly 1890, 264–95.
145. See below, pp.98–9.
146. Anon., *The Pedigree of the Penn Family* (1871) 23.
147. For these families, see above, n.68. The Cholmleys, Constables, Londesboroughs and Wenlocks were involved in Chancery suits over their settlements, according to the surviving archives and reported cases. *In re Lord Hotham's Trusts* [1871] 12 L.R.Eq. 76–7 is not concerned with a disputed settlement.
148. See below, p.50.
149. Kerly 1890, 271 gives an annual average number of bills filed in Chancery 1737–56 and in the 1820s, as 2150. 1225 bills were filed in 1801 (Kerly gives no figures for 1800).
150. Some other cases mention a strict settlement but are concerned with leasehold property, or stocks and shares.
151. Reports by Francis Vesey Jun., reprinted in *English Reports* XXXI (1903) contain Chancery cases for 1800.
152. For many examples see White and Tudor 1910, I 315–38, II 992–1059. Waste is discussed above, p.28.
153. Bond 1964, 325–6.
154. Clifford 1885–7, I (1885) 450–1.
155. Lists of private acts can be found in Bramwell 1813, and in *Index to Local and Personal Acts, 1801–1947* (HMSO 1949). From 1592 to 1714 the parliamentary papers relating to private bills and acts are calendared in the appendices to the *Reports* of the HMC and *Manuscripts of the House of Lords* (new series) I–XII. Different stages of the bills are reported in the *Lords Journals* and the *Commons Journals*. Additional material can be found among the House of Lords archives, in such sources as 'Committee Proceedings' which may include information not otherwise recorded. Works on private bills and acts include Williams 1954, Bond 1964, Lambert 1971, and Habakkuk 1980.
156. The process of obtaining a private act is described by Bond 1964 and Lambert 1971.
157. *Lords Journals: Commons Journals* (both 1800). The total number of alterations exceeds 25, because some acts were for more than one purpose. 1800 was taken to enable a

Notes 158–85 for pages 51–8 (for abbreviations and short titles see pp.116, 132–40)

comparison to be made with Chancery cases (p.49 above); the year was chosen at random, from the middle of the period of strict settlement.

158. For a discussion of the Settled Estates Act of 1856, see Thompson 1974, 173–9.
159. Underhill 1901; Spring, D. 1963; Spring, E. 1977.
160. Clifford 1885–7, I (1885) 403, 410. Other cases are cited in Stone 1977, 39.
161. See below, pp.69–70.
162. *H. of Lords MSS* NS XII (1977) 472.
163. Spring, E. 1964, 220.
164. Based on papers in the Downe archives, at North Yorkshire County Record Office (hereafter NYCRO).
165. Thompson 1955, 37.
166. Bateman 1883, 263. For the Coke family, see also Stirling 1908; Stirling 1913; James 1929; Parker 1975; Martins 1980. We are indebted to Dr W. O. Hassall and Mrs C. Hiskey for information from the archives at Holkham, and to Dr G. R. C. Davis and the National Register of Archives for permission to use H. A. Davidson's catalogue of the Holkham archives.
167. *HMC 11th Report app. pt II, H. of Lords MSS 1678–1688* (1887) 115. John Coke senior made a settlement in 1660 but revoked it in 1661 by a deed 'that is now eaten up by Ratts': NRA catalogue, Holkham Family Deeds (hereafter HFD) no.25.
168. 29 & 30 Ch.II c.8 (private).
169. 29 & 30 Ch.II c.8 (private).
170. HFD nos. 28, 28a; *HMC 12th Report app. pt VI, H. of Lords MSS 1689–1690* (1889) 254–5.
171. HFD nos. 28b, 31, 32, 33.
172. HFD nos. 33b, 33d; 29 & 30 Ch.II c.8 (private); *H. of Lords Journals 1675–1681*.
173. *HMC 11th Report app. pt II, H. of Lords MSS 1678–1688* (1887) 115; *HMC 12th Report app. pt VI, H. of Lords MSS 1689–1690* (1889) 253–4.
174. *Cal. S.P. Dom. 1696*, 155. Warrants of this kind do not seem to have been commonly issued, although the entry cited here is preceded in the calendar by a similar warrant for an under-age baronet.
175. HFD nos. 36, 37d. A draft of the marriage articles was printed by James 1929, 136–7.
176. NRA catalogue, Holkham, General estate deeds no.47.
177. HFD no.43.
178. HFD no.42. The private act of 20 Geo. II c.3 recites much of the settlement. For the lands left out of settlement, see Parker 1975, 29.
179. 20 Geo. II c.3 (private); Parker 1975, 29.
180. HFD no.56b.
181. Parker 1975, 191.
182. 25 Geo. III c.11 (private); 48 Geo. III c.175 (private); 52 Geo. III c.177 (private). Coke also settled land from his own fee simple estate on his brother Edward and his family and enlarged this settlement when his brother's son reached the age of 21, for this young man was the heir apparent to the Norfolk estates until a son was born to Coke in 1822. HFD nos. 73, 74, 85, 102, 109a, 109b, 109c.
183. 6 Vict. c.2 (private).
184. HFD nos. 128, 129, 131.
185. 6 Vict. c.2 (private); HFD nos. 126, 129, 145; will of the 2nd earl (d.1909) unclassified, at Holkham estate office; summary of the will supplied by Mrs C. Hiskey.

Notes 186–212 for pages 58–68 (for abbreviations and short titles see pp.116, 132–40)

186. Will of the 2nd earl, unclassified, Holkham estate office.
187. Gatty 1921, I 188–9.
188. This account of the Grosvenor settlement of the London estate is based throughout on the private acts of 27 Ch.II c.2 and 9 Anne c.22; *House of Lords MSS* NS IX (1949) no.2758; Cokayne 1910–59, XII pt ii (1959); Gatty 1921; Survey of London 1977; Huxley 1965; Huxley 1967.
189. 9 Anne c.22 (private); *H. of Lords MSS* NS IX (1949) no.2758.
190. Huxley 1967; Survey of London 1977, 48.
191. Bateman 1883, 228. The family archives are in HUL DDHO.
192. HUL DDHO/71/5.
193. HUL DDHO/71/7; 74/9 and 10.
194. For the Hothams at this period, see Roebuck 1980, 70–1.
195. HUL DDHO/58/8, 9; 71/8.
196. HUL DDHO/58/8, 9; 71/9, 12. She also granted some future rights to her son John, but revoked them the following year.
197. HUL DDHO/58/8, 9; 71/10.
198. HUL DDHO/29/4.
199. HUL DDHO/74/13.
200. Advice on this disentailing was given to the Hothams by a famous conveyancer Gilbert Horsman, author of *Precedents in Conveyancing* (1744). The brief for Horsman's opinion is a useful statement of the earlier settlement history of the estates: HUL DDHO/58/8, 9.
201. Roebuck 1980, 88.
202. HUL DDHO/70/20, 22, 23. Sir Charles's land, later described as unsettled (DDHO/20/26) was acquired subsequently, for the 1724 settlement encompassed the whole of the estate at the time of marriage; details of land purchased after 1724 are given by Roebuck 1980, 88–91.
203. They were so described in 1757, when they were charged with a jointure on the 6th baronet's marriage (HUL DDHO/71/31) and also so described in his will.
204. It was in the drawer of a Pembroke table in the Hothams' London house: HUL DDHO/17/11, 76–8. The will is recited in HUL DDHO/71/37.
205. HUL DDHO/71/36, 37.
206. 'Very doubtful' was the phrase used of this type of process in the foremost precedent book of the early nineteenth century, Bythewood and Jarman 1821–36, X (1833) 376, 404, 409n. However courts looked favourably on what they termed 'family arrangements' if all the existing interested parties were in agreement: in the event this disentailing was never challenged.
207. HUL DDHO/71/37.
208. HUL DDHO/70/39.
209. *In re Lord Hotham's Trusts* [1871] 12 L.R.Eq. 76–7.
210. HCCRO Registry of Deeds NA/303/472 and MQ/398/577; abstract of will also in HCCRO DDCC/43/264; *In re Lord Hotham's Trusts* [1871] 12 L.R.Eq. 76–7.
211. It is not known under precisely what conditions the 5th baron held the estates, as papers relating to the later settlement history of the estates are not available for study, but it can be deduced from the terms of the 3rd baron's will and the 4th baron's resettlement that the 5th baron was a life tenant under the 1872 deed.
212. For the Downing family and the history of the estates, see Stevens 1899; Cuttle and MacKenzie 1936; VCH, *County of Cambridge* III (1959) 487; French 1978. We are

Notes 213–30 for pages 68–74 (for abbreviations and short titles see pp.116, 132–40)

grateful to the Master and Fellows of Downing College and particularly to Mr Stanley French, archivist to the college, for assistance with the archives and permission to quote from them.

213. The marriage settlement is abstracted in Downing College muniments 69/3.
214. The will is in Downing College muniments parcel 74.
215. No disentailing has been found, nor is one mentioned in the abstracts of title. Recoveries were suffered in 1716, but these were primarily concerned with the disentangling of the marriage of the 3rd baronet; they may have also served to disentail the 1683 settlement. After 1711, as tenant in tail in possession, the 3rd baronet had no real restriction on his estates. For the 2nd baronet's difficulties, see French 1978.
216. The original will is in Downing College muniments 74/20. It was printed by Cuttle and MacKenzie 1936. The act of administration is in the PRO, PROB 6/88.
217. Downing College muniments 69/3: date from watermark of paper.
218. As the couple were under age, a private act would have been necessary to make a binding settlement at the time of marriage. It appears from the private act of 4 Geo. I c.17 that the only right the 3rd baronet's wife could have claimed in her husband's estate was the common law right of dower; this strengthens the view that there was no marriage settlement.
219. Documents relating to this transaction are in Downing College muniments, parcels 69 and 150. The act is entitled 'An Act for making more effectual certain articles of agreement between Sir George Downing Baronet and Dame Mary eldest daughter of Sir William Forester Knight and her trustees', 4 Geo. I c.17; further details in *Lords Journals* XX 45, 602, 603, 629, 663; *H. of Lords MSS* NS XII (1977) 500. The history of the separation is given in detail by French 1978, 18–26.
220. That there was a fee simple in 1716 is apparent from the abstract of title in Downing College muniments, parcel 70.
221. The will is printed by Stevens 1899, 256–68. The approximate acreage of the estate is calculated from French 1978, 31.
222. The history of the lawsuit is given in much greater detail in Stevens 1899 and French 1978. See also *Attorney General* v. *Lady Downing* (1767) Wilm. 1–35.
223. This account is based on the archives of the Bower family at HCCRO, class DDBR and at NYCRO, class ZFY. It has not been possible to put the settlement pattern into the tabular form used elsewhere in this chapter.
224. For the Lowthers see Beckett 1975, esp. ch. 6–9, and Beckett 1981. Also two articles by Bouch, 1942 and 1944, and Phillips 1979. These works contain more detailed pedigrees than that on pp.76–7. The estate acreage is from Bateman 1883, 279.
225. The Lowthers of Lowther, Whitehaven, Maulds Meaburn and Swillington all descended from Sir Christopher Lowther of Lowther, d.1572; Beckett 1978, 47.
226. Cumbria CRO, D/Lons/L/Wills/16 with a codicil of 1699.
227. Cumbria CRO, D/Lons/L/Lo.4/14. It does not seem from the grandfather's will that he exercised this power to leave a fee simple: D/Lons/L/Wills/9.
228. Cumbria CRO, D/Lons/L/Wills/16 and 47.
229. Beckett 1980, 133–4. A copy of the deed of settlement of 13 Feb. 1701 is in Cumbria CRO, D/Lons/L/Wills/23.
230. He had made earlier wills in 1698 (which had disinherited the elder in favour of the 2nd son) and 1702 (which confirmed the 1701 settlement); Cumbria CRO, D/Lons/L/Wills/15, 24. The final will of 1705 is D/Lons/L/Wills/16 and was printed by Jackson

Notes 231–50 for pages 74–85 (for abbreviations and short titles see pp.116, 132–40)

1888, 355–8.

231. Jackson 1888, 356. The reference is to the unborn tenant in tail.
232. Cumbria CRO, D/Lons/L/Wills/30. Associated papers (e.g. D/Lons/L/Wills/28, 29) show that James made other agreements with his elder brother to consolidate his position.
233. Excepting only burgage plots in Cockermouth.
234. Called in the will 'Sir James Lowther of Lowther' as he had by 1754 inherited the Lowther estates.
235. Copies or abstracts of the will in Cumbria CRO, D/Lons/L/Wills/40, 47. Details of the will and the resulting law suit are recorded in *Lowther* v. *Cavendish* (1758) 1 Eden 99–119. The trustees of the fund were the two heirs, William and James Lowther, and also Robert Harper of Lincoln's Inn, a notable conveyancer: for his career, see Lambert 1971. It seems likely from his inclusion that Harper drew up the will.
236. Sir William left his own unsettled estate of Holker by will to Lord George Cavendish (in strict settlement) and his estate at Marske to the Wilsons of Dallam Tower (as tenants in common and their heirs in survivorship): Cumbria CRO, D/Lons/L/Wills/41; Bouch 1944, 116, gives an over-simplified account of this partition.
237. *Lowther* v. *Cavendish* (1758) 1 Eden 99–119.
238. His fortune was said to be £2 million: Cokayne 1910–59, VIII (1932) 134.
239. An abstract of the will is in Cumbria CRO, D/Lons/L/Lo.1/30; also abstracted by Brydges 1812, 714–16, and summarised by Cokayne 1910–59, VIII (1932) 135. See also 43 Geo. III c.99 (private).
240. Cumbria CRO, D/Lons/L/Wills/44, dated 1787 with codicil of January 1788. Clearly the other uses, which are not specified, empowered the Revd William Lowther to devise the lands.
241. The act 43 Geo. III c.99 (private) related the settlement history from 1787 to 1803. The act was obtained to rationalise the holding of the Yorkshire estates.
242. This is deduced from the private act of 43 & 44 Vict. c.3. However property was still being settled to the uses of the 1801 will of James, 1st earl of Lonsdale as late as 1863: Cumbria CRO D/Lons/L/Box 5/9, 10, 13.
243. A copy of the will is at the Borthwick Institute York, proved 25 June 1844.
244. The 1855 settlement is abstracted in the Lonsdale Settled Estates Act (1880), 43 & 44 Vict. c.3 (private). The son of Henry Lowther was born in Oct. 1855, too late to be included as yet another life tenant in the settlement of Jan. 1855, so he eventually inherited as tenant in tail.
245. 43 & 44 Vict. c.3 (private), which also gives the settlement history from 1844 to 1880.
246. Sutherland 1965, 44. The papers of the 5th earl known as the 'Yellow Earl' are not open to researchers at present (1981).
247. Sutherland 1965, 80. The quotation (by Sutherland) is from the *Northern Counties Gazette*.
248. This account is based on the archives at NYCRO, ZDS and at HCCRO, DDCL/930–1049; see also an article by Perry 1976. The private act affecting the Wykeham Abbey estates was 43 Geo. III c.100; some papers relating to the Langleys are in HCCRO DDCL/747–766.
249. Bateman 1883, 137.
250. Some families' settlements of the late seventeenth and eighteenth centuries are described in Habakkuk 1980; for the settlements from c.1780 of the Fitzwilliams, the Percys and the Lambtons see Spring, E. 1964.

Notes 251–72 for pages 85–91 (for abbreviations and short titles see pp.116, 132–40)

251. HCCRO DDCC/111/283.
252. HCCRO DDCC/139/29.
253. Based on documents in HCCRO DDCC.
254. NUL Ne D 1, Ne L 1853; Turberville 1938–9; Davies 1965; Kelch 1974; Trumbach 1978, 47–50; Cokayne 1910–59, IX (1936). The eighteenth-century settlements in this family are better recorded than those of the nineteenth century. In 1870 the duke became bankrupt and transferred his life interest to a relative.
255. NUL Mi F, Mi 3 G and Mi 4 G; also Ne D 410-11; Trumbach 1978, 45; Cokayne 1910–59, VIII (1932). The eighteenth-century position is not well documented: titles given by nineteenth-century lawyers always start with the 1793 will. The 5th Lord Middleton complained that drink and gout had in great measure destroyed the preceding barons and perhaps they were not good at keeping their archives (NUL Mi F 12). The nineteenth-century Yorkshire and Lincolnshire estates settlement pattern was different from that of the Nottinghamshire lands, being not settled, or not settled for so long a period, by the 1793 will but settled in 1835, disentailed in 1867 and resettled in 1876, at the same time as the Applecross estate in Scotland.
256. Cokayne 1910–59, X (1945) 256–7 nn.
257. Burke 1869, I 79–80.
258. Cannadine 1977, 624–50, and articles and books cited there, especially Stone 1965; also Mingay 1963; Thompson 1963.
259. Turner 1931; Simpson 1961, ch.x; Mingay 1976, 114; Habakkuk 1979 and 1980.
260. Maguire 1974, 15.
261. Brodrick 1881, 116–17, regarded post-obit bonds as a major cause of encumbrance on estates, owing to the very high interest rates demanded by the money lenders. If the terms of the post-obit bonds were thought to be unfair ('catching bargains') Chancery would give relief against the penalties. See *Chesterfield* v. *Janssen* (1750–1) 2 Ves. Sen. 125–60, and the legal discussion centred on this case in White and Tudor 1910, I 303–46.
262. Lists of encumbrances on estates can be found among family archives; for instance, those on the Burton Constable estates in the late nineteenth century are in HCCRO DDCC/139/62. There are lists of the encumbrances of the nineteenth-century dukes of Bedford in Spring, D. 1963, 189–90.
263. The affairs of the duke of Buckingham are discussed below, pp.98–9.
264. Until 1861, only people involved in certain trades could be made bankrupt; other people were technically 'insolvent debtors'. It was, however, very common to talk of bankruptcy among the landed gentry; for instance, the duke of Wellington in 1847 named three noblemen driven to bankruptcy: Spring and Spring 1956, 174.
265. NUL Ne L 1853. The 7th duke, son of the bankrupt duke, died in 1928. His will was proved provisionally at £1,000,000; Cokayne 1910–59, XI (1936) 537.
266. See pp.36, 98
267. See p.27.
268. Mingay 1963, 37; Cannadine 1977.
269. English 1982.
270. NUL Mi 4 G 7.
271. *House of Lords MSS* NS XII (1977) 374.
272. Kelch 1974; Survey of London 1977; Cokayne 1910–59, V (1926) 296 and Verney 1892–9, I (1892) 16–18; Thompson 1958; Spring, D. 1956–7, 472–4. Such trusteeships

Notes 273–301 for pages 91–106 (for abbreviations and short titles see pp.116, 132–40)

were only concerned with the life interest of the life tenant, and perhaps the remainderman if he agreed to join; the trustees of the emergency situation had no power to alter the settlement itself. In an emergency of this kind the trustees might be involved in a considerable amount of work: those of the 2nd duke of Kingston for a time met every day; Mingay 1963, 48–9, 67–70.

273. Spring, D. 1951, 18.
274. See above p.51.
275. Verney 1892–9, I (1892) 16–18; *DNB* XX (1899), 265–6, account of Lord Verney by M. M. Verney. Other examples of families that failed in the eighteenth century are given in Habakkuk 1980.
276. Mingay 1963, 125–30; Burke's *Landed Gentry* (various editions).
277. Burke 1869, I 307–12.
278. Private acts 22 Ch. II c.9 and 8 Wm III c.34 (manuscript acts in the House of Lords Record Office); *House of Lords MSS* NS II (1903) 136–8; Hodgson 1893–1935, IV (1897) 329–50; Hedley 1968–70, II (1970) 48–62.
279. 22 Ch. II c.9 (private).
280. 22 Ch. II c.9 (private).
281. He was tenant in tail because he had been born after the 1675 settlement.
282. 8 Wm III c.34 (private).
283. Hedley 1968–70, II (1970) 58.
284. Hedley 1968–70, II (1970) 58.
285. Hodgson 1893–1935, IV (1897) 348.
286. The account of the marquis of Ailesbury's troubles is taken from *In Re Marquis of Ailesbury's Settled Estates* [1891] 1 Ch.D. 506–48; *Law Reports Appeal Cases* (1892) 356–66; *Law Times* NS LXV (1892) 409–13, 830–7; *Law Times* NS LXVII (1893) 490–3; Cardigan 1949. Where there are differences between the sources (for example Lord Cardigan gives a different account of the settlement of the Yorkshire estates) the legal sources have been preferred.
287. Thompson 1963, 331–2.
288. 'Nimrod' c.1869; Burke 1869, I, 332–44.
289. Burke 1869, II 333; Rumbold 1902, II 75–8; Wood 1954, 65–81.
290. Thompson 1955; Spring and Spring 1956.
291. Thompson 1955, 48. After the disentailing, the position became more complicated, for it would have been possible for the mortgagees to sell off their different interests in the estates, and yet not raise enough money to pay off all the outstanding debts: Spring and Spring 1956, 184.
292. It used to be considered that an estate of 10,000 acres was needed to maintain a major country house; Culme-Seymour 1974, 140.
293. Bythewood and Jarman 1821–36, X (1834) 369.
294. HCCRO DDSA/641.
295. See above, p.57.
296. Spring 1964, 217–18.
297. Nottingham Univ. Lib. Mi 4 G 8/3.
298. See above, p.85.
299. Cumbria RO, D/Lons/L/Wills/47.
300. PP 1829, 6; quoted, Holdsworth 1927, 305.
301. Article 'Agriculture', *Enyclopaedia Britannica* II (1842) 342.

Notes 302–28 for pages 106–15 (for abbreviations and short titles see pp.116, 132–40

302. Humphreys 1826; Thompson 1963, 65–6 and ch.1 n.28 above.
303. C. P. Villiers, for example, in a House of Commons debate (10 June 1845) noted that 'the owner of land is tenant for life and the occupier is tenant-at-will; and these are precisely the conditions under which it is most unfavourable to good agriculture that the land should be held'; Villiers 1883, II 240.
304. Morley 1906, 521–2.
305. 15 Sept. 1855.
306. 24 Nov. 1855.
307. Morley 1906, 920.
308. For a brief discussion, Clapham 1926–38, II (1932) 252–3; and for a more detailed, contemporary account, Brodrick 1881, 157–97.
309. John Bateman published four editions: the most useful was the last, which appeared in 1883.
310. Brodrick 1881, 165.
311. Dewey 1974; Martin 1982.
312. Fowler 1880. The literature, especially the pamphlet literature, was voluminous. Joseph Kay, *Free Trade in Land* (1883) was a much-read book. See also Arnold 1880, and the cross-examination of Arnold (who was MP for Salford) by the R.C. on Agriculture (the Richmond Commission) during which Arnold, who was a fervent advocate of the small owner-occupier, was shown to be ill-informed on a number of matters of central importance to the general argument, including that of settlement: PP 1882, Qs 63144–863 (15 and 16 Dec. 1881).
313. Dicey 1905, 221–32.
314. See, for example: *Will Socialism benefit the British People?: verbatim report of a debate between H. M. Hyndman and Charles Bradlaugh* (1884) 40pp.
315. Cannadine 1977, 650.
316. Sturmey 1955, 245–68; Offer 1981, chs. 4, 5 and 17.
317. Douglas 1976; Offer 1981, *passim.*
318. Habakkuk 1939–40, 2.
319. Thompson 1957; Thompson 1966; Thompson 1969.
320. Habakkuk 1965.
321. Thompson 1969.
322. Clay 1968; Beckett 1977.
323. Habakkuk 1953, 2.
324. Habakkuk 1979, 190.
325. Bonfield 1979.
326. Caird 1878, 87.
327. Cannadine 1977, 649.
328. Thompson 1965.

Bibliography and Short Titles of Works cited in the Notes

Abel-Smith and Stevens 1967	B. Abel-Smith and R. Stevens, *Lawyers and the Courts* (1967)
Adelson 1975	R. Adelson, *Mark Sykes* (1975)
Arnold 1880	A. Arnold, *Free Land* (1880)
Aveling 1960	H. Aveling, *Post-Reformation Catholicism in East Yorkshire* (1960)
Barlow 1957	A. C. H. Barlow, 'Gifts and other Transfers Inter Vivos and the Matrimonial Home', in R. H. Graveson and F. R. Crane eds, *A Century of Family Law 1857–1957* (1957) 197–226
Bateman 1883	J. Bateman, *Great Landowners of Great Britain and Ireland* (1883)
Beastall 1975	T. W. Beastall, *A North Country Estate. The Lumleys and Saundersons as Landowners, 1600–1900* (1975)
Beckett 1975	J. V. Beckett, 'Landownership in Cumbria c.1690–c.1750' (Lancaster Univ. Ph.D, 1975)
Beckett 1977	J. V. Beckett, 'English Landownership in the Later Seventeenth and Eighteenth Centuries: the debate and the problems', *Econ. Hist. Rev.* 2nd ser. XXX (1977) 567–81
Beckett 1978	J. V. Beckett, 'The Lowthers at Holker: marriage, inheritance and debt in the fortunes of an eighteenth-century landowning family', *Hist. Soc. of Lancs. & Ches.* 127 (1978) 47–64
Beckett 1980	J. V. Beckett, 'The Disinheritance of Sir Christopher Lowther in 1701', *C. & W.A. & A.S.* NS LXXX (1980) 131–6
Beckett 1981	J. V. Beckett, *Coal and Tobacco: the Lowthers and the economic development of West Cumberland, 1600–1760* (1981)
Birks 1960	M. Birks, *Gentlemen of the Law* (1960)
Blackstone 1765–9	W. Blackstone, *Commentaries on the Laws of England*, 4 vols (1765–9)
Blundell 1952	M. Blundell, ed., *Blundell's Diary and Letter Book 1702–1728* (1952)
Bond 1964	M. Bond, 'Estate Acts of Parliament', *History* NS XLIX (1964) 325–8
Bonfield 1978	L. J. Bonfield, 'Marriage Settlement 1601–1740: the development and adoption of the strict settlement' (Cambridge Univ. Ph.D, 1978)
Bonfield 1979	L. J. Bonfield, 'Family Settlements and the "Rise of Great Estates": the demographic aspect', *Econ. Hist. Rev.* 2nd ser. XXXII (1979) 483–92
Bonfield 1981	L. J. Bonfield, 'Marriage Settlements, 1660–1740' in R. B. Outhwaite, ed., *Marriage and Society* (1981) 101–16
Boswell 1970	J. Boswell, *Life of Johnson* ed. R. W. Chapman and J. D. Fleeman (1970)
Bouch 1942	C. M. Lowther Bouch, 'Lowther of Swillington from its Origin till 1788', *C. &. W.A. &. A.S.* NS XLII (1942) 67–102
Bouch 1944	C. M. Lowther Bouch, 'Lowther of Marske (Cleveland) and Holker', *C. & W.A. &. A.S.* NS XLIV (1944) 100–18
Bowring 1843	J. Bowring, ed., *Collected Works of Jeremy Bentham* V (1843)
Bramwell 1813	G. Bramwell, *Analytical Table of the Private Statutes, 1727–1812* (1813)
Bridgeman 1682, 1689	*Sir Orl. Bridgman's Conveyances: being select precedents of deeds and instruments concerning the most considerable estates in England* vol. I (1682), vol. II (1689), further editions (1702) and (1725)

Bibliography

Brodrick 1881	G. C. Brodrick, *English Land and English Landlords* (1881)
Brydges 1812	S. E. Brydges, ed., *Collins' Peerage of England* V (1812)
Burke 1869	B. Burke, *The Vicissitudes of Families* 2 vols (1869)
Bythewood and Jarman 1821–36	W. M. Bythewood and T. Jarman, *Conveyancing* 11 vols (1821–36)
Caird 1878	J. Caird, *The Landed Interest and the Supply of Food* (1878)
Cannadine 1977	D. Cannadine, 'Aristocratic Indebtedness in the Nineteenth Century: the case re-opened', *Econ. Hist. Rev.* 2nd ser. XXX (1977) 624–50
Cardigan 1949	The Earl of Cardigan, *The Wardens of Savernake Forest* (1949)
Carr-Saunders and Wilson 1933	A. M. Carr-Saunders and P. A. Wilson, *The Professions* (1933)
Clapham 1926–38	J. H. Clapham, *An Economic History of Modern Britain* 3 vols (1926–38)
Clay 1968	C. Clay, 'Marriage, Inheritance and the Rise of Large Estates in England, 1660–1815', *Econ. Hist. Rev.* 2nd ser. XXI (1968) 503–18
Clifford 1885–7	F. Clifford, *A History of Private Bill Legislation* 2 vols (1885, 1887)
Cokayne 1910–59	G. E. Cokayne et al., *The Complete Peerage* 13 vols (1910–59)
Coke 1832	*Coke upon Littleton* (1832)
Cooper 1976	J. P. Cooper, 'Inheritance and Settlement by Great Landowners' in J. Goody, J. Thirsk and E. P. Thompson eds, *Family and Inheritance* (1976) 192–327
Crane 1957	F. R. Crane, 'Family Settlement and Succession' in R. H. Graveson and F. R. Crane eds, *A Century of Family Law 1857–1957* (1957) 227–55
Culme-Seymour 1974	M. Culme-Seymour, 'The House and the Estate' in R. Strong, M. Binney, J. Harris eds, *The Destruction of the Country House* (1974) 139–41
Cuttle and MacKenzie 1936	W. L. Cuttle and K. W. S. MacKenzie, 'A Will made by Sir George Downing Second Baronet on 15th September, 1688', *Downing Muniments* II (1936)
Davies 1965	O. R. F. Davies, 'The Wealth and Influence of John Holles, Duke of Newcastle 1694–1711', *Renaissance and Modern Studies* IX (1965) 22–46
Davidson 1844–85	C. Davidson et al., *Davidson's Precedents and Forms in Conveyancing* 5 vols (1844–85)
Dewey 1974	C. Dewey, 'The Rehabilitation of the Peasant Proprietor in Nineteenth-Century Economic Thought', *History of Political Economy* 6 (1974) 17–47
Dicey 1905	A. V. Dicey, 'The Paradox of the Land Law', *Law Q. Rev.* XXI (1905) 221–52
Douglas 1976	R. Douglas, *Land, People and Politics: a history of the land question in the United Kingdom, 1878–1952* (1976)
Ellis 1974	R. Ellis, 'The Muniment Room', in R. Strong, M. Binney, J. Harris eds, *The Destruction of the Country House* (1974) 133–5
Elphinstone 1900	H. W. Elphinstone, *Introduction to Conveyancing* (1900)
English 1982	B. A. English, 'On the Eve of the Great Depression: the economy of the Sledmere estate 1869–1878', *Business History* XXIV (1982) 24–47
Farran 1958	C. D'O. Farran, *The Principles of Scots and English Land Law* (1958)
Farwell 1874	G. Farwell, *A Concise Treatise on Powers* (1874)

Fearne 1772 — C. Fearne, *Essay on the Learning of Contingent Remainders and Executory Devises* (1772)

Finch 1956 — M. E. Finch, *Five Northamptonshire Families 1540–1640* (1956)

Fowler 1880 — W. Fowler, *Limited Ownership of Land. Remarks on the Committee of the House of Lords on Improvement of Land, 1873* (1880)

French 1978 — S. French, *The History of Downing College Cambridge* (1978)

Gatty 1921 — C. T. Gatty, *Mary Davies and the Manor of Ebury* 2 vols (1921)

Gover 1889 — W. H. Gover, *Advising on Title* (1889)

Habakkuk 1939–40 — H. J. Habakkuk, 'English Landownership, 1680–1740', *Econ. Hist. Rev.* X (1939–40) 2–17

Habakkuk 1950 — H. J. Habakkuk, 'Marriage Settlements in the Eighteenth Century', *TRHS* 4th ser. XXXII (1950) 15–30

Habakkuk 1953 — H. J. Habakkuk, 'England' in A. Goodwin ed., *The European Nobility in the Eighteenth Century* (1953) 1–21

Habakkuk 1965 — H. J. Habakkuk, 'La Disparition du paysan anglais', *Annales ESC* 20 (1965) 649–63

Habakkuk 1979 — H. J. Habakkuk, 'The Rise and Fall of English Landed Families', *TRHS* 5th ser. 29 (1979) 187–207

Habakkuk 1980 — H. J. Habakkuk, 'The Rise and Fall of English Landed Families 1600–1800: II', *TRHS* 5th ser. 30 (1980) 199–221

Habakkuk 1981 — H. J. Habakkuk, 'The Rise and Fall of English Landed Families 1600–1800: III', *TRHS* 5th ser. 31 (1981) 195–217

Harding 1966 — A. Harding, *A Social History of English Law* (1966)

Harvey 1973 — B. W. Harvey, *Settlements of Land* (1973)

Hayes and Jarman 1863 — W. Hayes and T. Jarman, *Concise Forms of Wills* (1863)

Hedley 1968–70 — W. P. Hedley, *Northumberland Families* 2 vols (1968–70)

Hodgson 1893–1935 — J. C. Hodgson et al., *History of Northumberland* 14 vols (1893–1935)

Holdsworth 1922–57 — W. S. Holdsworth et al., *History of English Law* 17 vols (1922–57)

Holdsworth 1927 — W. S. Holdsworth, *Historical Introduction to the Land Laws* (1927)

Hollingsworth 1964 — T. Hollingsworth, 'The Demography of the British Peerage', *Population Studies* XVIII (1964)

Humphreys 1826 — J. Humphreys, *Observations on the Actual State of the English Laws of Real Property* (1826)

Huxley 1965 — G. Huxley, *Lady Elizabeth and the Grosvenors* (1965)

Huxley 1967 — G. Huxley, *Victorian Duke: the life of Hugh Lupus Grosvenor, first Duke of Westminster* (1967)

Jackson 1888 — W. Jackson, 'Some Account of Sir John Lowther, Baronet, of Whitehaven, from Original Sources', *C. & W.A. & A.S.* IX pt ii (1888) 333–59

James 1929 — C. W. James, *Chief Justice Coke, his Family and Descendants at Holkham* (1929)

Kay 1883 — J. Kay, *Free Trade in Land* 7th ed. (1883)

Kelch 1974 — R. A. Kelch, *Newcastle, a Duke without Money* (1974)

Kenny 1878 — C. S. Kenny, *The History of the Law of Primogeniture in England* (Cambridge, 1878)

Kenny 1879 — C. S. Kenny, *The History of the Law of England as to the Effects of Marriage on Property and on the Wife's Legal Capacity* (1879)

Kerly 1890 — D. M. Kerly, *History of Equity* (1890)

Lambert 1971	S. Lambert, *Bills and Acts* (1971)
Lewin 1928	T. Lewin, *Lewin on Trusts* ed. W. Banks (1928)
Lewis 1937–81	W. S. Lewis, ed., *Horace Walpole's Correspondence* 42 vols (1937–81)
Lightwood 1929	J. M. Lightwood, 'Trusts for Sale', *Camb. Law J.* III (1929) 59–74
Maguire 1974	W. A. Maguire, *Letters of a Great Irish Landlord* (1974)
Maitland 1911	F. Maitland, 'The Law of Real Property', *Collected Papers* I (1911) 162–201
Margerison 1886	S. Margerison ed., 'Memorandum Book of Sir Walter Calverley', in *Yorkshire Diaries,* Surtees Soc. LXXVII (1886)
Martin 1982	D. E. Martin, *John Stuart Mill and the Land Question,* Univ. of Hull Occasional Papers in Economic and Social History no. 9 (1982)
Martins 1980	S. W. Martins, *A Great Estate at Work. The Holkham Estate and its Inhabitants in the Nineteenth Century* (1980)
Maxwell and Maxwell 1955	W. H. Maxwell and L. F. Maxwell, *A Legal Bibliography of the British Commonwealth of Nations* 2 vols (1955)
Mendelson and Slater 1979	S. H. Mendelson and M. Slater, 'Debate', *Past and Present* 85 (1979) 126–40
Mingay 1963	G. E. Mingay, *English Landed Society in the Eighteenth Century* (1963)
Mingay 1976	G. E. Mingay, *The Gentry* (1976)
Morley 1906	J. Morley, *Life of Richard Cobden* (1906)
'Nimrod' *c.*1869	'Nimrod', *The Life of John Mytton Esq. of Halston Shropshire* 4th ed. (*circa* 1869)
North 1826	R. North, *Lives of the Norths* 3 vols (1826)
Offer 1981	A. Offer, *Property and Politics 1870–1914* (1981)
Park 1833	J. J. Park, *Systems of Registration, and Conveyancing: a lecture delivered at King's College, London, October 30th, 1832* (1833)
Parker 1975	R. A. C. Parker, *Coke of Norfolk* (1975)
Perry 1976	J. Perry, 'The Dawnay Archive', *NYCRO Journal* 4 (Northallerton, 1976) 93–110
Phillips 1979	C. B. Phillips, ed., *Lowther Family Estate Books,* Surtees Soc. CXCI (1979)
Pollock 1883	F. Pollock, *The Land Laws* (1883)
Pollock 1896	F. Pollock, *The Land Laws* (1896)
Powell 1787	J. J. Powell, *An Essay . . . of Powers* (1787)
PP 1829	Parliamentary Papers, *First Report of the Commissioners of Inquiry into the Law of England respecting Real Property,* 1829 (263) X
PP 1833	Parliamentary Papers, *Fourth Report of the Commissioners of Inquiry into the Law of England respecting Real Property,* 1833 (226) XXII
PP 1875	Parliamentary Papers, *Return of Owners of Land, 1873* (England and Wales) 1874 LXXII pt II [C.1097–I], published in 1875
PP 1881	Parliamentary Papers, *Royal Commission on Depressed Condition of the Agricultural Interests,* 1881 [C.3096] XVII
PP 1882	Parliamentary Papers, *Royal Commission on Depressed Condition of the Agricultural Interests,* 1882 [C.3309–I] XIV
Riddall 1979	J. G. Riddall, *Introduction to Land Law* (1979)
Robson 1959	R. Robson, *The Attorney in Eighteenth-Century England* (1959)
Roebuck 1980	P. Roebuck, *Yorkshire Baronets 1640–1760* (1980)
Rubinstein 1981	W. D. Rubinstein, *Men of Property* (1981)
Rumbold 1902	H. Rumbold, *Recollections of a Diplomatist* 2 vols (1902)

Simpson 1961	A. W. B. Simpson, *Introduction to the History of the Land Law* (1961)
Slater 1976	M. Slater, 'The Weightiest Business: marriage in an upper-gentry family in seventeenth-century England', *Past and Present* 72 (1976)
Smith 1928	G. C. Moore Smith, *Letters of Dorothy Osborne to William Temple* (1928)
Spring D. 1951	D. Spring, 'The English Landed Estate in the Age of Coal and Iron: 1830–1880', *J. of Economic History* XI (1951) 3–24
Spring D. 1963	D. Spring, *The English Landed Estate in the Nineteenth Century* (Baltimore, 1963)
Spring, D. and E. 1956	D. Spring and E. Spring, 'The Fall of the Grenvilles', *Huntington Lib. Q.* 19 (1956) 165–90
Spring E. 1964	E. Spring, 'The Settlement of Land in Nineteenth-Century England', *Amer. J. of Legal History* 8 (1964) 209–23
Spring E. 1977	E. Spring, 'Landowners, Lawyers and Land Law Reform in Nineteenth-Century England', *Amer. J. of Legal History* 21 (1977) 41–59
Squibb 1959	G. D. Squibb, 'The End of the Name and Arms Clause?' *Law Q. Rev.* 69 (1959) 219–25
Stevens 1899	H. W. P. Stevens, *Downing College* (1899)
Stirling 1908	A. M. W. Stirling, *Coke of Norfolk and his Friends* 2 vols (1908)
Stirling 1913	A. M. W. Stirling, *The Letter Bag of Lady Elizabeth Spencer Stanhope* 2 vols (1913)
Stone 1965	L. Stone, *Crisis of the Aristocracy 1559–1641* (1965)
Stone 1977	L. Stone, *Family, Sex and Marriage* (1977)
Sturmey 1955	S. G. Sturmey, 'Owner Farming in England and Wales, 1900 to 1950', *Manchester School of Economic and Social Studies* XXIII (1955) 245–68
Sugden 1808	E. B. Sugden (Lord St Leonards), *A Practical Treatise of Powers* (1808)
Sugden 1858	E. B. Sugden (Lord St Leonards), *A Handy Book of Property Law* (1858)
Sugden 1861	E. B. Sugden (Lord St Leonards), *A Practical Treatise of Powers* (1861)
Survey of London 1977	Survey of London, *The Grosvenor Estate in Mayfair* pt I, vol. XXXIX of Survey (1977)
Sutherland 1965	D. Sutherland, *The Yellow Earl* (1965)
Thirsk 1969	J. Thirsk, 'Younger Sons in the Seventeenth Century', *History* LIV (1969) 358–77
Thompson 1955	F. M. L. Thompson, 'The End of a Great Estate', *Econ. Hist. Rev.* 2nd ser. VIII (1955) 36–52
Thompson 1957	F. M. L. Thompson, 'The Land Market in the Nineteenth Century', *Oxford Economic Papers* NS 9 (1957) 285–308
Thompson 1958	F. M. L. Thompson, 'English Landownership: the Ailesbury Trust 1832–56', *Econ. Hist. Rev.* 2nd ser. XI (1958) 121–32
Thompson 1963	F. M. L. Thompson, *English Landed Society in the Nineteenth Century* (1963)
Thompson 1965	F. M. L. Thompson, 'Land and Politics in England in the Nineteenth Century', *TRHS* 5th ser. 15 (1965) 23–44
Thompson 1966	F. M. L. Thompson, 'The Social Distribution of Landed Property in England since the Sixteenth Century', *Econ. Hist. Rev.* 2nd ser. XIX (1966) 471–86
Thompson 1969	F. M. L. Thompson, 'Landownership and Economic Growth in

England in the Eighteenth Century' in E. L. Jones and S. J. Woolf eds, *Agrarian Change and Economic Development* (1969) 41–60

Thompson 1974 — F. M. L. Thompson, *Hampstead: building a borough 1650–1964* (1974)

Thomson 1937 — G. Scott Thomson, *Life in a Noble Household* (1937)

Trumbach 1978 — R. Trumbach, *The Rise of the Egalitarian Family* (1978)

Turberville 1938–9 — A. S. Turberville, *A History of Welbeck Abbey and its Owners* 2 vols (1938–9)

Turner 1931 — R. W. Turner, *The Equity of Redemption* (1931)

Tyrer and Bagley 1968–72 — F. Tyrer and J. Bagley eds, *The Great Diurnal of Nicholas Blundell,* 3 vols, Record Soc. of Lancs. and Ches. 110 (1968), 112 (1970), 114 (1972)

Underhill 1901 — A. Underhill, 'Changes in the Law of Real Property', in *A Century of Law Reform* (1901) 280–340

Verney 1892–9 — F. P. Verney, *Memoirs of the Verney Family* 4 vols (1892–9)

Villiers 1883 — C. P. Villiers, *The Free Trade Speeches of Charles Pelham Villiers, M.P.* 2 vols (1883)

White and Tudor 1910 — F. T. White and O. W. Tudor, *Leading Cases in Equity* 2 vols (1910)

Williams, J. 1858 — J. Williams, 'On the Origin of the Present Mode of Family Settlements of Landed Property', *Papers of the Juridicial Society* I (1858) 45–67

Williams, J. 1862 — J. Williams, 'Transfer of Land', *Papers of the Juridicial Society* II (1862) 589–628

Williams, J. 1879 — J. Williams, *The Settlement of Real Estates* (1879)

Williams, O. C. 1954 — O. C. Williams, *The Clerical Organization of the House of Commons, 1661–1850* (1954)

Wood 1954 — A. C. Wood, 'George, Lord Rancliffe', *Trans. of Thoroton Soc. of Notts.* LVIII (1954) 65–81

Wylie 1975 — J. C. W. Wylie, *Irish Land Law* (1975)

Glossary

ABSTRACT OF TITLE A chronological summary of the deeds and other documents constituting the title to an estate.
ADMINISTRATION The settling of the affairs of a deceased person who died without leaving a valid will; the administrator was granted 'letters of administration'.
ALIENATE To transfer property away from one person to another.
APPOINTMENT *see* General Power of Appointment.
ARTICLES OF AGREEMENT An agreement between parties, intended to be formalised later in a settlement: often the basis of a marriage settlement. See p.36.
ASSURANCE A deed conveying property.
ATTAINDER Extinction of civil rights when a person was convicted of treason or felony.
BAR To destroy (of entail or of common law right of dower).
BASE FEE The fee created by a tenant in tail, not in possession, who barred the entail for himself and his own issue.
BEQUEST Personal property left by will; a legacy.
CODICIL Postcript to a will.
COMMON RECOVERY *see* Recovery.
CONTINGENT REMAINDER A remainder (in an entail) that might happen but was not certain: for example, a remainder to a child that might be born but did not exist at the time.
CONVEYANCE The transfer of property, or the deed by which this was recorded.
CROSS REMAINDER If the heirs of one estate died out, by this arrangement the heirs of another estate might inherit, and vice versa. See p.33.
DEVISE To leave by will, particularly used of real estate.
DISENTAIL To end (destroy) the entail.
DOCK To end (destroy) the entail.
DOWER Property or income settled on a woman at marriage by her husband's family, to be enjoyed by her during widowhood. Also her common law right to ⅓ of her husband's property.
DOWRY Property or money brought by a bride from her family to her bridegroom's family.
ENCUMBRANCE *see* Incumbrance
ENTAIL A limited succession established by settlement.
EQUITY A body of law, distinct from common law, administered by the Lord Chancellor and intended to moderate the flaws in the common law.
ESTATE ACT Private act of Parliament passed to make or alter a settlement. See pp.49–52.
ESTATES (DOCTRINE OF) Various interests in lands were called estates. Land, or property, could be divided like a cake, with many different people owning or possessing different rights in it: these were different estates.
FEE SIMPLE An interest in property limited to a man and his heirs: the nearest to absolute ownership that the law recognised.
FEE TAIL An interest in property limited to a man and the heirs of his body: also called an estate tail. *See also* Tail General, Tail Male.
FINE Legal document which ended a fictitious lawsuit, often used to end an entail. A fine was 'levied'.
GENERAL POWER OF APPOINTMENT One of a number of powers that could be included in a settlement. A general power of appointment was equivalent to a power of revocation. See pp.29–30.
HEIRLOOMS Chattels (such as prized furniture or pictures) included in a settlement to follow the descent of the estate.
HOTCHPOT The throwing together of property into a single fund for distribution: in a

settlement, the hotchpot clause may direct that advances made by the life tenant to his children in his lifetime are to be taken into account in determining their final shares. See p.27.

INCUMBRANCE A charge upon an estate.

INTESTATE One who died without leaving a valid will.

ISSUE Children born of the person named.

JOINTURE Property settled on a woman at marriage by her husband's family, to be enjoyed by her during widowhood.

LIFE ESTATE, LIFE INTEREST The right of a person to hold property for life.

LIFE TENANT A person who held property for life only.

MAJORITY Coming of age: until 1969, legally this happened at 21.

MORTGAGE Conveyance of real estate as security for a loan.

PERSONALTY Personal property (as opposed to real estate).

PIN-MONEY A sum paid periodically by a husband to his wife for her personal use.

PORTION Capital sum assigned to younger children.

POST-NUPTIAL SETTLEMENT Settlement on a couple after their marriage, made in consideration of the marriage.

POWER Authority to do some particular thing, especially used of authority granted in a settlement, such as power to grant leases, to mortgage or to make exchanges.

PRECEDENT Example that might be followed: particularly a model conveyance.

PRE-NUPTIAL SETTLEMENT Settlement on a couple before their marriage, made in consideration of their marriage.

PRIMOGENITURE Until 1926, the right of the eldest son to succeed to property if his parent died intestate. See p.24.

PROBATE Notification that a will has been proved (accepted) in the appropriate court.

REAL ESTATE, REALTY Equivalent to property in land (as opposed to personalty).

RECOVERY OR COMMON RECOVERY A fictitious law suit, which ended an entail or other encumbrance on land. A recovery was 'suffered'.

REMAINDER An interest in land which began at the end of a previous interest; a future interest.

REMAINDERMAN A person entitled to an estate in remainder.

REVERSION A future interest which derived from the determination of a grant: but often used of any future interest, in remainder or in reversion.

SEPARATE ESTATE Property enjoyed by a married woman through a trust set up for her use, separate from her husband's rights. See p.32.

SETTLED ESTATE Property under settlement: the estate refers to interests in the land, not as in the present meaning of 'landed estate'.

SETTLEMENT The transaction of arranging the transmission of property: the deed or set of deeds by which the succession to land was subject to limitations. See p.11.

STRICT SETTLEMENT A settlement which restricted succession to certain persons.

TAIL GENERAL An interest in land limited to a person and the heirs of either sex of his or her body.

TAIL MALE An interest in land limited to a person and the heirs male of his body (tail female was a possible interest but in practice did not occur: special tail could restrict the inheritance to the heirs of a particular couple).

TENANT FOR LIFE *see* Life Tenant.

TENANT IN TAIL The next in succession after all previous life tenancies named in a settlement had ended. Tenants in tail could be 'expectant' or 'in possession'.

TENURE The manner in which property was held.

TRUST The interest of a person who is invested with property or rights for the benefit of another.
TRUSTEE A person to whom an estate is conveyed in trust for another.
USE From the Statute of Uses (1535), equivalent to a trust.

The glossary is based on J. B. Saunders, ed. *Mozley & Whiteley's Law Dictionary* 9th ed. (1977) and J. Burke, ed. *Jowitt's Dictionary of English Law* 2 vols (1977).

Index